# NATO AND
THE ATLANTIC DEFENSE

# NATO AND THE ATLANTIC DEFENSE

Perceptions and Illusions

Werner J. Feld
John K. Wildgen

PRAEGER SPECIAL STUDIES • PRAEGER SCIENTIFIC

**Library of Congress Cataloging in Publication Data**

Feld, Werner J.
  NATO and the Atlantic defense

  Includes index.
  1. North Atlantic Treaty Organization.
I. Wildgren, John K.   II. Title.   III. Title: N.A.T.O.
and the Atlantic defense.
UA646.3.F44          355'.031'091821          81-22676
ISBN 0-03-059477-4                            AACR2

Published in 1982 by Praeger Publishers
CBS Educational and Professional Publishing
A Division of CBS, Inc.
521 Fifth Avenue, New York, New York 10175 U.S.A.

© 1982 Praeger Publishers

*All rights reserved*

23456789   145   987654321

Printed in the United States of America

# ACKNOWLEDGMENTS

Books written at leisure often require the authors to obtain help from others. This text was written quickly; instead of seeking more help, we had to make outright impositions in some cases. The North Atlantic Treaty Organization supported part of our work through its fellowship program and through the helpfulness and personal generosity of Fernand Welter of the NATO Press and Information Secretariat. Kenneth Adler and Douglas Wertman of the United States International Communications Agency (USICA) provided us with the benefit of their insights into European public opinion and assisted us in getting USICA raw data. Wally Miller of the National Archives provided us with essential guidance in unscrambling the complexities of the physical records gathered by several European polling organizations. Leonard Wood, executive vice-president of the Gallup Organization, provided us with additional tabulations. The University of New Orleans Research Council and the University of New Orleans Computer Research Center also provided material assistance to the conduct of the study.

The data utilized in this book were made available in part by the Interuniversity Consortium for Political and Social Research. Neither the collectors of the data nor the Consortium bear any responsibility for the analyses or interpretations presented here. The CBS News Archives also made available transcripts of CBS broadcasts pertaining to NATO. Archive director Sam Saratt provided invaluable assistance and much insight into the network news industry.

Among the most imposed-upon persons involved in completing the manuscript were Jan Davis, who provided not only unparalleled typing services but also the benefit of her extensive copyediting experience, and Betsy Brown, Praeger's tireless and supportive political science editor. Finally, we also extend thanks to our wives Betty and Kathy who understand so well the art of making life go on pleasantly while books are in progress.

New Orleans, August 31, 1981
Werner J. Feld    John K. Wildgren

# CONTENTS

| | | |
|---|---|---|
| Acknowledgments | | v |
| List of Tables, Figures, and Exhibit | | ix |
| 1 | FROM THE "DEFI AMERICAIN" TO THE "DEFI SOVIETIQUE" | 1 |
| | The Tattered Umbrella | 3 |
| | Life under the Umbrella | 8 |
| | Soviet Security and Economic Concerns | 15 |
| | The Impact of Public Opinion | 18 |
| | Notes | 20 |
| 2 | THE PUBLIC IMAGE OF NATO IN THE UNITED STATES | 22 |
| | Print Media and Television | 22 |
| | Public Information | 23 |
| | Pipelines Input and Output | 24 |
| | NATO Coverage of Seven Newspapers | 25 |
| | NATO Coverage by Newsmagazines | 31 |
| | NATO in April 1978: A Comparative Analysis of Two U.S. Media | 33 |
| | Conclusions | 43 |
| 3 | THE IMPACT OF NATO-PRODUCED FILMS | 45 |
| | A Test of a NATO Film | 52 |
| | Summary and Conclusions | 61 |
| 4 | PUBLIC OPINION ABOUT DEFENSE AND NATO AND MEDIA INFLUENCE | 65 |
| | U.S. Foreign Policy Attitudes and Constituencies | 66 |
| | Commitment to Defense | 74 |
| | Commitment to NATO | 79 |
| | The Role of the Media | 85 |
| | Summary and Conclusions | 87 |
| | Notes | 89 |

| | | |
|---|---|---|
| 5 | EURODOVES AND EUROHAWKS | 90 |
| | Some Technical Comments | 90 |
| | Perceptions of Power: At Present and in the Future | 96 |
| | The Path to European Security | 98 |
| | The European Commitment to Defense | 102 |
| | A Trend toward Finlandization? | 106 |
| | The Factor of U.S. Resolve | 107 |
| | The Influence of Party Affiliation | 111 |
| | The Influence of Other Socioeconomic Indicators | 112 |
| | Party Influences on the Continent | 115 |
| | The Progression of Western Europe's Public Opinion Pattern | 120 |
| | Conclusions | 123 |
| | Notes | 123 |
| 6 | POLICY IMPLICATIONS | 125 |
| | The Linkage between Public Opinion and Policy | 125 |
| | NATO Policies under Disapproval | 127 |
| | Divisive Issues | 130 |
| | Transatlantic Policy Disparities: Are There Any Solutions? | 135 |
| | Policy Coordination and Reconciliation | 140 |
| | Suggestions for the Future | 143 |
| | Notes | 145 |
| APPENDIX A: | Certification of Telecasts | 147 |
| APPENDIX B: | Questionnaire | 153 |
| APPENDIX C: | Should the U.S. Supply Military Force if the Soviet Union Attacked . . . | 161 |
| INDEX | | 167 |
| ABOUT THE AUTHORS | | 173 |

## LIST OF TABLES, FIGURES, AND EXHIBIT

| Table | | Page |
|---|---|---|
| 1.1 | Comparative Technological Innovation in Offensive Strategic Weapons | 9 |
| 2.1 | Monthly Totals of NATO Newspaper Stories | 28 |
| 2.2 | Comparison of Publication of NATO-Related Articles | 31 |
| 2.3 | NATO Coverage by Major Newsmagazines | 32 |
| 2.4 | Calendar of News Events Covered by *New York Times* and CBS News, April 1978 | 36 |
| 3.1 | Responses to Political Evaluation and National Spending Priority Questions | 54 |
| 3.2 | Responses to Philosophical Questions on War | 58 |
| 3.3 | Responses to NATO-Related Questions | 59 |
| 3.4 | Cognition of Allies | 60 |
| 3.5 | Cognition and Defense: NATO-Related Issues | 62 |
| 4.1 | Distribution of Foreign Policy Constituency Types, 1973 to 1980 | 71 |
| 4.2 | The Relationship between Education and Foreign Policy Constituency Groups | 72 |
| 4.3 | The Relationship between Partisanship and Foreign Policy Constituency Groups | 72 |
| 4.4 | Changes in U.S. Feelings toward NATO: A Growing Commitment | 80 |
| 4.5 | The U.S. Commitment to NATO | 81 |
| 4.6 | The Use of Military Force in the Event of Soviet Intervention | 82 |
| 4.7 | The Defense of the Persian Gulf Region | 84 |
| 4.8 | The Ambiguous Role of the Media I: Interest in Foreign News in the Press and Commitment to NATO | 85 |
| 4.9 | The Ambiguous Role of the Media II: Hours of TV Exposure and Feelings about Defense Spending | 86 |
| 4.10 | Public Attentiveness and Percent Wanting to Expand Defense Spending: The Impact of the Media | 87 |

| 5.1 | The Most Powerful Nation at Present | 96 |
| --- | --- | --- |
| 5.2 | The Most Powerful Nation in Five Years | 97 |
| 5.3 | Is NATO or the Warsaw Pact Stronger? | 98 |
| 5.4 | The Comparative Strength of NATO and the Warsaw Pact in Five Years | 98 |
| 5.5 | What Is the Best Way to Provide Security? | 99 |
| 5.6 | Maximum Security and Perceptions of National Power: Great Britain | 101 |
| 5.7 | Maximum Security and Perceptions of National Power: Germany | 101 |
| 5.8 | Maximum Security and Perceptions of National Power: France | 101 |
| 5.9 | The Level of Military Expenditures | 104 |
| 5.10 | The Geographic Limits for NATO | 105 |
| 5.11 | Confidence in U.S. Resolve to Defend Europe | 108 |
| 5.12 | The Impact of Party Affiliation in Britain | 111 |
| 5.13 | The Impact of Occupation | 112 |
| 5.14 | The Impact of Education Based on Age that Schooling Was Completed | 113 |
| 5.15 | The Impact of Social Class by Self-Categorization | 114 |
| 5.16 | The Impact of Union Membership | 115 |
| 5.17 | Partisanship and Neutralism in Britain: How Perceptions of U.S. Commitment Play a Role | 115 |
| 5.18 | Confidence in the United States and Neutralist Tendencies: Evidence from Three Allies | 116 |
| 5.19 | Major French Political Parties and Strategic Outlook, 1980 | 117 |
| 5.20 | Preferred Security Arrangement by Political Party Supported, April 1980 | 118 |
| 6.1 | Percentage Change in NATO Defense Spending from Previous Year in Constant Prices | 128 |
| 6.2 | Preferred Foreign Policy Arrangement by Country, April 1980 | 141 |

Figure

| | | |
|---|---|---|
| 2.1 | *New York Times* NATO Coverage, 1977 to 1978 | 42 |
| 2.2 | CBS News NATO Coverage, 1977 to 1978 | 42 |
| 2.3 | Combined CBS News and *New York Times* NATO Coverage, April 1978 | 43 |
| 3.1 | Newspaper Coverage, 1977 to 1978 | 47 |
| 3.2 | 1978 Showings of *The Great Highway* | 48 |
| 3.3 | 1978 Showings of *Borealis* | 49 |
| 3.4 | 1978 Showings of *Europe and America* | 50 |
| 3.5 | 1978 Showings of New Version of *Europe and America* | 51 |
| 4.1 | A Typology of Foreign Policy Attitudes | 70 |
| 4.2 | Feelings about Other Nations | 73 |
| 4.3 | Selected Spending Priorities, 1973 to 1980 | 76 |
| 4.4 | The United States Changes Its Mind about Defense | 76 |
| 4.5 | The Generations and Spending Priorities | 78 |
| 4.6 | Selected Spending Priorities, 1973 to 1980 | 78 |
| 5.1 | Percentage of GNP Spent on Military, 1969 to 1978 | 103 |
| 5.2 | Power, Confidence, and the Eurodoves | 109 |
| 5.3 | Expected Shifts in Military Balance, March-April 1981 | 121 |
| 5.4 | Influence of United States and Soviet Union on World Events, March-April 1981 | 122 |

Exhibit

| | | |
|---|---|---|
| 5.1 | Multiregional Security Survey Questionnaire: West Europe | 92 |

# NATO AND
THE ATLANTIC DEFENSE

# 1

# FROM THE "DEFI AMERICAIN" TO THE "DEFI SOVIETIQUE"

Through the expenditure of billions of dollars, the American and European publics have supported an alliance that is now a generation old. In numerous bases, airfields, caserns, and posts, the assorted forces of the North Atlantic Treaty Organization (NATO) are now manned by personnel young enough in some cases to be grandchildren of World War II veterans. The Western alliance is a remarkably enduring collective effort on the part of many nations, some of whom had been bitter enemies for centuries prior to the establishment of NATO.

On the economic front, the basis of the alliance lies on three pillars: the Marshall Plan that rebuilt Europe, American private investment in Europe through U.S. multinationals, and now European private investment in the United States through European multinationals. Thirty years ago Europe was the United States' poor cousin. Now, in aggregate, it enjoys a rough parity in standard of living. In individual cases, some European nations are richer than the United States. In any event, up to the present time, the economic ties between Europe and the United States have been mutually rewarding.

Another tie in the alliance is political. It is sometimes hard to distinguish politics from culture or economics. But the alliance is based on a common feeling that NATO is a democratic club in an era when democracy is an endangered species in the community of nations. Not all NATO members have avoided sliding into dictatorship from time to time (Greece, Turkey), but the overall commitment is there, if only in a negative sense. After all, NATO is an anti-Soviet, antitotalitarian alliance.

In spite of the reassuring historical background, the Atlantic defense relationship may well be put to the test during the 1980s. At least during the early part of the decade, the alliance is likely to face a period of severe turbulence. The tough stand assumed by the Reagan administration toward the Soviet Union seems to be backed by American public opinion. Detente has lost its luster for both the U.S. government and its people, although it is unclear how much acceptance it ever gained when one remembers President Ford's banning the term during his 1976 presidential campaign.

For the West Europeans, the perception of the *defi Americain* (American challenge), economic and otherwise, which produced so much discomfort and annoyance during the late 1960s and early 1970s, has been pushed to the background by views of U.S. economic and military decline, particularly during the Carter presidency. In spite of the Soviet invasion of Afghanistan and the change in views vis-à-vis the United States, perceptions of a *defi Sovietique* (Soviet challenge) by the West Europeans do not appear to have assumed a major significance. Overriding West European concerns with continued and perhaps increasing trade with communist Europe, symbolized by detente no matter how undermined by suspicions of Soviet intentions, have carried the day and concomitantly provided assurances of an expanding job market. On the other hand, although deplored in some quarters, the U.S. government and people accepted a sharp reduction of trade with the Soviet Union, including a temporary grain embargo, as a proper means to curb Soviet adventurism and expansionism.

Aggravating the disparity of interests, views, and priorities is the issue of sharing the burden for the common defense. Americans resent carrying the major share (and tax burden) for paying for the weapons and personnel needed to present a credible defense posture, although they have accepted it since World War II. The West Europeans recognize the problem, often try to rationalize it in terms of the United States' global leadership and responsibilities versus their own more limited role, and promise on occasion to do better. Unfortunately, their promises are not always fulfilled.

The West Europeans and sometimes the Canadians have complaints of their own. They feel that U.S. leaders at times ignore their special interests, do not adequately consult them before taking important military or economic actions, and use the alliance to promote—if not impose—the sale of American-produced weapons and equipment. The West Europeans would especially like to see a more equitable military procurement policy that would assure appropriate and fair benefits to arms and equipment manufacturers in all NATO countries provided, of course, that their products meet the necessary standards and are competitive in price.

There are also areas of disagreement regarding strategic doctrines, conceptual gaps on how to deal with the Soviet Union and its satellites as well as with East-West relations in general, and differences of views across the Atlantic on economic and monetary policies. All this points to dilemmas for the Atlantic relationship in general and NATO in particular that require attention and, if possible, solution. But finding solutions is made all the more difficult by perceptions and images that both policymakers and the public have about each other in different NATO countries—perceptions that often are misperceptions when, for example, West Germany's Chancellor Schmidt believes that Americans are uninformed and misunderstand German problems. False perceptions, perhaps based on traditional but incorrect assumptions and images, may, in turn, create illusions about the character and powers of a particular NATO ally and its people that could be damaging to the common efforts of the alliance.

Through an analysis and evaluation of relevant public opinion data and by content analysis of selected newspapers in the United States, this book will attempt to shed light on this vast and sometimes contradictory array of perceptions, misconceptions, and illusions that have arisen in connection with NATO and the Atlantic defense. These data will be used to project trends of decisions that may be made by policymakers in major NATO countries with respect to the viability of NATO, the solidarity of the common defense, and East-West relations in general. The authors are, of course, fully aware that expressions of public opinion cannot be translated directly into what individual governments will or will not do. They fully understand the fragility of establishing a nexus between such data and future policy. But by identifying and carefully taking into account the particular interests of individual member states, certain inferences can be drawn regarding the probable behavior individual governments may manifest and the courses of action they may seek to pursue within the context of what, in their view, needs to be done to deal with the *defi Sovietique*.

## THE TATTERED UMBRELLA

For more than a generation, Western Europe and the United States have sought security from the Soviet threat through an alliance that conveyed to Soviet authorities the notion that the West had the will and the necessary means to defend itself. NATO, then, became a weave of perceptions and realities that, in their complementarity, formed an adequate structure for deterrence. The centerpiece of this structure was and remains the U.S. nuclear arsenal, which constitutes a "nuclear umbrella" over Europe.

Yet there are now widespread doubts about both perceptions of American will and realities of American nuclear and conventional capabilities. This volume will take up both topics. However, at the outset, it must be pointed out that part of the basis for the erosion of confidence in the United States—and the resulting concern over the "Finlandization" of Europe—lies in a decade of U.S. misperceptions of the Soviet Union and the nature of the strategic contest between the two powers.

Since the beginning of the Kennedy administration, U.S. strategic thought has undergone several iterations. The "massive retaliation" notions of the Eisenhower-Dulles era have been replaced by notions of "flexible response" and "countervailing strategy," and nuclear superiority has given way to "parity" and "sufficiency." These labels have been glued to an old bottle with old wine: the wine of "assured destruction."

Assured destruction or, better, "mutually assured destruction," is a strategy based on the axiom that nuclear war is irrational and unthinkable, but that the United States would be provoked into participating in such a conflict by a Soviet attack on either the United States or Europe. It is a deterrent, indeed, an extended-deterrent strategy quite at odds with present knowledge of Soviet thinking on nuclear war.[1]

What can be said in favor of assured destruction is that it has worked in a negative sense in that the Soviets have not attacked. Mutually assured destruction (sometimes abbreviated with the unfortunate acronym MAD), for all its presumed success, does not have too many open advocates. The reason for the lack of advocacy lies in the fact that the logic of assured destruction basically says: "I won't attack you because if I do you will retaliate with surviving forces against my population—but if you attack I will retaliate against your population." When the attack under discussion is nuclear, assuring the deaths of millions, the deterrent force of MAD is based on mutual hostage holding. This makes almost all strategists a bit queasy.

As queasy as they might be, some strategists are still apologists for MAD and show scant sympathy for alternative approaches. As George Rathjens and Jack Ruina point out, "We know of no advocates of assured destruction, but we know many who believe that, since we have an assured destruction capability, we need very little else."[2]

Why is very little else needed than a strategy that holds populations hostage and promises the equivalent of national suicide upon sufficient provocation, such as an attack on West Germany, the Netherlands, or Paris? The first answer is obvious: if the Soviets believe, for a moment, in what the United States says, they will not risk an attack. But this is only the first of several assumptions Americans have made about Soviet leadership that support a strategy of assured destruction. The others can be listed briefly:

1. Once a nation has an assured destruction capability, additional weapons are useless and wasteful. Numbers do not count.

2. Building additional weapons only spurs the other side to respond with more weapons. The arms race fits a stimulus-response positive-feedback model.

3. As a consequence of (2), the Soviet Union will match U.S. restraint arms acquisition. The Soviets appreciate reciprocal-initiative arms control logic.

4. Failing (1), (2), and (3), the United States should not become concerned because it has a qualitative edge over the Soviet Union.

These notions, either singly or in toto, are hard to support in the light of the strategic situation of the 1980s. First, it has become questionable how far the Soviet Union's strategic thinkers remain impressed by the logic of mutually assured destruction. Reviews of their literature stress not deterrence but war-fighting and war-winning approaches.[3]

Second, Europeans, as well, have expressed uneasiness at the credibility of the United States' extended deterrent and the will to use it. In a sense, U.S. notions of assured destruction had, as a secondary purpose at least, an arms control and limitation goal. Ironically, these goals provided an excuse for nuclear proliferation. Responding to U.S. critiques of the French nuclear arms program, President de Gaulle observed:

> It is quite true that the number of nuclear weapons with which we can equip ourselves will not equal, far from it, the mass of those of the top giants of today. But since when has it been proved that a people should remain deprived of the effective weapons for the reason that its chief possible adversary and its chief friend have means far superior to its own?[4]

Assured destruction, then, while a basic doctrine that was relied upon as an effective deterrent by the United States during the 1960s and 1970s when it had a monopoly or vast superiority in weaponry, is being questioned now by some Europeans and Americans and may be rejected by the Soviets.

Some of the other ideas associated with assured destruction thinking have been discredited or completely disproven by events. The wish that "numbers don't count" has been harshly treated by events. Former Secretary of Defense James Schlesinger once lamented to a Senate subcommittee:

> You will recall that there were hopes some years ago that when the Soviets reached a deployment of approximately a thousand ICBM's they would cease construction of new silos, they would level off their forces as we had leveled off our forces 5 or 6 years previously, and then both sides would be satisfied with something that appeared to be numerical parity. I think there was widespread disappointment that the Soviets did not choose to level off. Obviously their guideposts for the sizing and composition of their forces happened to be different from ours, or at least different from ours in that period of time.[5]

Schlesinger's admission lays to rest the "numbers don't count" argument as far as the USSR is concerned. Obviously, numbers do count for the Soviets. Why, though, have they adopted such a different guidepost? Some good clues are provided by Edward N. Luttwak:

> With a consistency that would be remarkable if it were accidental, Soviet force structure decisions have tended to maximize the perceptible manifestations of Soviet military power, while an equally consistent neglect of perceptual factors is evident in the character of American force structures.[6]

It is certainly true that the Pentagon has for years emphasized the sophistication of U.S. arms and the crudeness of Soviet efforts. But Luttwak notes that the numbers of Soviet weapons make easy a form of perceptual manipulation that can be spread throughout the world to achieve political advantage. Even though mere numbers may not count in military terms per se, they certainly count in international politics.

The question of U.S. participation in a game of perceptual manipulation raises the spectre of the arms race spiral, resulting in costs and economic dislocations.[7] The argument that somehow Soviet defense expenditures are a dependent variable of U.S. measures is a simplistic, almost vulgar model that has long been discredited.[8] But, like the legendary phoenix, the arms spiral argument keeps rising from its own ashes in the U.S. strategic community in a pernicious, one-sided form. On the one hand, U.S. plans for weapons deployment are denounced for being provocative (or environmentally harmful). Yet provocative Soviet deployments are glossed over or rationalized. In a critique of the halfhearted and tentative NATO decision to allow deployments of U.S. ground-launched cruise missiles (GLCM) and the Pershing II battlefield support missile, Kevin N. Lewis wrote:

> The recent controversy was set off by what has been perceived as an abrupt shift from a long-standing state of inertia in the area of intermediate-range systems resulting from the deployment by the USSR of greatly improved intermediate-range missiles and bombers. Some comparatively vulnerable Russian missiles installed almost 20 years ago are in the process of being replaced and augmented by what seems to be a much superior system, the mobile SS-20 missile, which carries three independently targetable nuclear warheads. In addition, an advanced Russian medium-range bomber, the TU-26 (code-named Backfire by NATO intelligence agencies), has been entering service in growing numbers.[9]

One might think that this certainly is support for the arms spiral hypothesis: action produces reaction. But Lewis sees no justification, political or military, for a U.S. reaction save in one instance: "Probably the only development that would make the new forces sufficiently attractive would be the possibility of promoting wide-ranging arms-control agreements on intermediate-range nuclear forces in Europe."[10]

The NATO counterdeployment of intermediate-range ballistic missiles (IRBMs) and GLCMs, according to Lewis, is a form of symptomatic relief that ignores "political and strategic causes of concern" between the United States and the Soviet Union.[11] He is not specific about what those concerns are, but one can guess that the United States and its allies are concerned about the SS-20's gratuitous deployment. Soviet concerns, one can guess as well, are that without the SS-20 it will have to find other means to intimidate Europe into compliance with Soviet objectives. There is very little here to negotiate. Still, it was not until the USSR was faced with the planned deployment of the Pershing II and the GLCM that Soviet authorities initiated token reductions of a few conventional force elements. Thus a NATO decision to acquire arms was matched by a Soviet concession (though no military expert views the Soviet moves as anything genuinely affecting Warsaw Pact strength).

On the other hand, the U.S. decision to not deploy the enhanced radiation warhead (the so-called neutron bomb) was not met by any form of Soviet counterrestraint. The warheads were not bombs but, instead, were designed to fit either Lance battlefield support missiles or eight-inch artillery tubes. Their mission was essentially as an antitank round that would minimize collateral damage to civilians near the battle zone.

The U.S. use of restraint in not deploying the warheads was certainly nudged along by fears in some quarters that the warheads, because of their limited collateral damage, would lower the nuclear threshold. The difficulty with this, however, is that the Soviets have not stopped deploying the T-80 tank, which appears quite resistant to NATO's family of conventional antitank weapons, including Tube-launched Optically-tracked Wire-guided antitank missiles (TOW), Dragon, Haute Optiquement téléguidé tiré d'un Tube (HOT), and Missile d'Infanterie Leger Antichar (MILAN) systems.[12] This leaves NATO with the uncomfortable dilemma of either allowing the passage of the T-80, or using current, high collateral damage warheads on them. This appears to be a case where weakness is more provocative than strength, and provides another example of where U.S. restraint has been unrequited by the USSR.

Still, there are few issues more genuinely debatable than the relative force strengths of U.S. and Soviet arms. The technical, tactical, operational, strategic, and political factors both countries face make one-to-one comparisons misleading. This kind of perfectly appropriate thinking has also led to a U.S. tendency to produce, in spurts, state-of-the-art systems in contrast to a steadier flow of continuously improving weapons as seems to be Soviet practice. Leon Gouré noted that "Even when the Soviets appear on the verge of acquiring the necessary capability for the conduct of effective strategic operations they continue to invest in the development of still more advanced systems."[13] But, as Gouré also notes, the United States has a great deal of confidence in its technological superiority.

In the overall evaluation of both economies and scientific establishments, there seems to be no contest, as a census of Nobel Prize contestants would suggest. But William H. Kincade has provided a stunning demonstration of how empty U.S. self-assurance of technological superiority in the military realm is (see Table 1.1). It may be that it is only in the military realm, as Luttwak suggests, that the USSR threatens assorted U.S. leads. But it is obvious that the Soviets made a commitment to match and excel current U.S. efforts in the military realm.

If it is the case that the United States cannot count on technical superiority, that the Soviets do not play a game of reciprocal initiative in arms acquisition, that weapons acquisition policies do fit a spiral model of interaction, that numbers of weapons do count, and that apparently the Soviets and some Europeans do not accept the philosophy of assured destruction, where does that leave the United States?

It seems that the U.S. strategy of assured destruction has been abandoned, at least on paper. In August 1980 Presidential Directive 59 committed the United States to a "counterforce" strategy in lieu of the "countercity" implications of MAD. This brings government policy, on paper, up to date with the mainstream of much strategic thinking. There is, however, a major difficulty. The counterforce strategy now adopted requires the targeting of hardened launch sites in the USSR with existing countercity weapons designed to have lethalities for soft targets. As long as the United States held to MAD, it developed weapons congruent with that strategy. It now appears the United States has, perhaps, a better (though strongly contested) strategy but lacks the weapons to implement it. That makes for a very tattered nuclear umbrella.

## LIFE UNDER THE UMBRELLA

For Europeans, life under the U.S. nuclear umbrella has been characterized by some rather restless chafing. In the years of the alliance prior to the dramatic advances in Soviet rocketry of the late 1950s, the most bothersome question was that of arming the Germans. Was it going to be possible to somehow create a German soldier who would fight for Europe instead of Germany? How could it be done in a manner satisfactory to Germany's recent enemies—especially the French? One hope was the European Defense Community, a complicated attempt to form a kind of supranational armed force. The idea was ill-fated, and eventually Germany was authorized rearmament within the context of the West European union and became a member of NATO.

As Europeans concentrated on economic growth, they were made aware of the U.S. concern that they were not paying enough attention to defense. From a European point of view, this made perfect sense. As they saw it, "the real deterrent to a Soviet threat lay in the nuclear dimension."[14] A nuclear

**TABLE 1.1: Comparative Technological Innovation in Offensive Strategic Weapons**

| Innovation | United States | Soviet Union |
| --- | --- | --- |
| Atomic (nuclear explosion) | 1945 | 1949 |
| Intercontinental bomber operational | 1948 | 1955 |
| Hydrogen (thermonuclear) explosion | 1951 | 1953 |
| Deliverable thermonuclear weapon | 1954 | 1955 |
| Nuclear-powered submarine | 1954 | 1958 |
| First test of intercontinental ballistic missile (ICBM) | 1958 | 1957 |
| Operational ICBM | 1960 | 1959 |
| Operational submarine-launched ballistic missile (SLBM) | 1960 | 1957 |
| Solid propellant ICBM operational | 1962 | 1968 |
| Test of multiple reentry vehicle (MRV) (U.S. deployment: 1964) | 1962 | 1968 |
| Test of multiple independently targetable reentry vehicle (MIRV) | 1968 | 1973 |
| ICBM with MIRVs operational | 1970 | 1974/75 |
| Test of modern long-range cruise missiles (ALCM, SLCM) | 1976 | 1979 (?) |
| High operational ICBM accuracy (CEP* approximately .15 nautical mile) | 1980 | mid-1980s |
| Antisatellite weapons | mid-1980s | mid-1980s |

*Circle of Equal Probability
Source: William H. Kincade, "Over the Technological Horizon," *Daedalus* (Winter 1981):124.

umbrella obviated the need, it was supposed, for conventional galoshes. But during the years of U.S. nuclear monopoly and superiority, Europeans were not without defense concerns. An effective deterrent meant a guarantee that in the event of a Soviet attack, the United States would strike at the Soviet heartland, rather than confine the battle to Western Europe. Consequently, weapons systems such as IRBMs were welcomed—as were U.S. troops. In a sense, both the weapons and the troops were hostage-like pledges of U.S. commitment.

This kind of visible commitment was especially important to the Germans and Benelux nations. The Italians were somewhat insulated by neutral Austria, deviationist Yugoslavia, and the Alps. The British still maintained a semblance of a "special relationship" with the United States in nuclear technology, while the French had begun, in the mid-1950s, to develop their own nuclear systems.

Once it became clear that the USSR deployed the systems necessary to directly strike the United States, the U.S. guarantee became more and more questionable. But the responses of various allies differed greatly. The most complicated, and complicating for the time being, were those of the French. The French attitude is of particular importance because part of it was unique, and another part set a tone that other allies later followed.

In February 1966 President de Gaulle was asked about German participation in NATO nuclear planning. He took the question as an opportunity to express three troubling ideas about the alliance that appear to plague it today. First de Gaulle noted:

> For it is quite clear that, owing to the internal and external evolution of the countries of the East, the Western world is no longer threatened today as it was at the time when the American protectorate was set up in Europe under the cover of NATO.

Then he went on:

> But, at the same time as the alarms were dying down, there was also a reduction in the guarantee of security—one might say absolute—that the possession of the nuclear weapon by America alone gave to the Old Continent, and in the certainty that America would employ it, without reservation, in the event of agression.

Subsequently he added:

> On the other hand, while the prospects of a world war breaking out on account of Europe are dissipating, conflicts in which America engages in other parts of the world—as the day before yesterday in Korea, yesterday in Cuba, today in Vietnam—risk, by virtue of that famous escalation, being extended so that the result could be a general conflagration.[15]

It is important to note the three basic premises here:

- The Soviet Union and its satellite system are evolving toward a peace-pursuing stance.
- U.S. security guarantees are unreliable.
- The United States itself poses a threat to peace and may drag Europe into war through its own adventurism.

These issues are not brought up to flail at the ghost of de Gaulle. From his record, it is known that he took these issues with a grain of salt. But why did he bring them up? Largely because he knew Europeans and what they could be led to believe or wanted to believe at their convenience. The difficulty is that these ideas, expressed in early 1966, are still widespread and may well be taken more literally than ever by important segments of European (and American) public opinion.

One should examine the notion of the evolution of the Soviet bloc. Little remains of de Gaulle's almost mystical vision of a Europe united from the Atlantic to the Urals (at least along voluntaristic lines). But European politicians appear to have an uncanny ability to dismiss Soviet muscle flexing and power projection, even when it threatens Europe. At the current time, NATO is outnumbered by a factor of 2.8 to 1 in armor, 2.2 to 1 in aircraft, 2.7 to 1 in artillery, and 1.2 to 1 in personnel. Furthermore, Europeans now have to confront the 3,000-mile range, triple MIRVed SS-20 mobile missile.[16] This listing excludes, of course, the growth of U.S.-targeted Soviet weaponry.

European intellectuals often regard themselves as having a more humanistic orientation than their opposite numbers in the United States. They frequently express disapproval of the kind of counting done in the paragraph above. In speaking to the U.S. Senate Foreign Relations Committee, Norway's Paul Thyness, president of the North Atlantic Assembly, made the following observations regarding SALT II:

> But apart from the tiny minority that specializes in the somewhat arcane world of strategic theory where the conclusions one reaches fairly often are of doubtful relevance in the affairs of living and breathing men, most Europeans are content to study the treaty in its broadest terms. These appear to indicate that SALT II does establish a position of "essential equivalence" where advantages for one side in certain areas are balanced by concessions in others. It is extremely difficult to see how, as some critics assert, the United States is moving into a position of strategic inferiority.

Yet, scarcely a breath later, he said:

> I think it must be accepted that over the last decade the military balance has tilted significantly in favor of the Warsaw Pact, leading to considerable uneasiness in most Western European countries.

It is possible to reconcile "essential equivalence" with a balance tilted "significantly in favor of the Warsaw Pact" in many ways. But Thyness chose to do so in a revealing way that explains much of the apparent contempt for facts:

> I am very much afraid that an adverse vote in the Senate will never really be understood in Europe. And when people do not understand something they become suspicious, and the explanations they make up are usually rather ungenerous, if not outright hostile and accusatory.
> If I had no other reason to support the treaty, this would have been enough.

In the end, Thyness summed up the European politicans' problem with defense and detente:

> We in Europe will be faced with a public opinion problem of staggering proportions, and no doubt the Soviet Union will work that for all it is worth.[17]

It is unfair, however, to pick on a lone Norwegian without pointing out that he is hardly alone in glossing over the facts of the Soviet arms buildup while hypnotized by the possibilities of detente. In a report on NATO growing out of a visit by four senators to Europe, one finds the following comment by the American travelers after listening to German government officials complain about delays in Senate ratification of SALT:

> It was clear, however, that their concern was based less on an appreciation for the substantive merits of the Treaty—indeed, most of the leaders demonstrated a superficial understanding of the technical content of the Treaty—than on the fact that the postponement as a political expression of United States policy would disrupt the dialogue and, thus, call into question the fundamental relationship of detente.[18]

It would be wrong to parody Europeans as guilty, in all cases, of the legendary behavior of the ostrich. No doubt, some of them really do believe a deal can be arranged with the USSR independently of that country's ability to employ military pressure. Furthermore, it would be misleading to ignore some European politicians on the left who genuinely admire the Soviet model.

But certain Europeans are quite good at counting and at taking sums in very shrewd ways that baffle Americans. These people are not so inclined to think that the USSR is interested only in defense, deterrence, and detente. They see it as a quite capable, threatening, military machine. Thus they have a genuine concern with the U.S. security guarantee. Their concern is that any outbreak of hostilities may not be confined to Western Europe. Rather, they seek an alliance structured so that U.S. involvement is absolutely guaranteed.

That is why the issue of Eurostrategic systems, or the virtually equivalent formulation of theater nuclear forces (TNF), is a matter of so much concern. True, the roughly 6,000 Soviet reentry vehicles targeted against U.S. land-deployed missiles gravely threaten U.S. second-strike capabilities. But to respond with one-for-one Eurostrategic weapons against a menace like the SS-20 raises the specter of nuclear warfare fought exclusively in Europe. The Europeans are caught in a dilemma. They cannot be totally reliant on vulnerable U.S.-based weapons to deter an attack on Europe; some credible theater nuclear forces are necessary. However, too many make possible an equally provocative decoupling of the U.S. and West European weapons.

There is a further iteration within the Eurostrategic debate. Americans see it as largely an intra-German debate, but it affects the common defense. In a 1977 speech to the Institute for Strategic Studies, Chancellor Schmidt raised the issue that the Germans feel they cannot be the sole host of the new TNF deployments.[19] The Soviets—as well as the German left—would regard this as a possible form of unilateral German revanchism. Thus other allies have to be brought into the picture, even though the weapons themselves may be better positioned from a technical viewpoint in Germany. In any case, some other likely countries for Pershing II deployment—such as Belgium, the Netherlands, Italy, Denmark, and Norway—seem to be able to muster one or more excuses to resist deployment on their own territory. The German reluctance to singularity in hosting TNFs is based on a fairly persuasive set of arguments backed up by angry Soviet statements on the topic. So how do these admittedly necessary weapons (necessary because of European doubts about U.S. reliability) get wedged into European sites when there is such reluctance to have them? The answer has been to play to the third of de Gaulle's complaints about the United States: its adventurism. Essentially, the idea has been to link eventual deployment of the Eurostrategic weapons to discussion with the Soviet Union on limiting these weapons.

Part of this may be a maneuver to satisfy public opinion. Evidence that the Soviets would actually be willing to agree to limits on the SS-20 is utterly lacking, even though they may be willing to talk about it on the condition that the West continues to delay its own deployments. But a link of development to talks in the offing could be a considerable sop to left-wing European public opinion.

What public opinion? This theme will be developed further. But basically, there is a sort of "Soviet dove" hypothesis abroad in Europe. The hypothesis, expressed by Schmidt in a Harvard address, is that "there are political elements [in the East] who are in favor of reconciliation and understanding with the West."[20] These elements, it is argued, would be weakened by Western toughness. In Germany, at least, few politicians pause to ask how much "Soviet hawks" have been validated in the eyes of their party by Western accommodations and appeasement in the face of Soviet rockets.

Instead, Soviet arms expenditures and adventures are blamed on the United States. Currently, it is en vogue to suggest that the Soviet invasion of Afghanistan can be attributed to Politburo frustration over U.S. delays in SALT II ratification. "The Soviets had nothing to lose," it is argued. Other rationalizations for Soviet behavior are offered as well. There seems to be a consensus in the German Social Democratic Party's left that Afghanistan is an area of traditional Russian influence that entitles the USSR to a fairly free hand there. Nevertheless, as Schmidt put it to a party conference held in Essen on June 9, 1980, "We do not stand between the camps in this conflict."[21] In view of the chancellor's clear position, Americans cannot be blamed if they find it an anomaly to see so much government and public handwringing in Germany over the dispatch to El Salvador of two dozen U.S. military advisers.

But where do Europeans get the notion that it is the United States, rather than the Soviet Union, that poses a threat to peace? It certainly cannot come from cases like El Salvador. There is something much deeper here, though not at all easy to understand. If one thinks back to 1977 and 1978, the views of many Europeans were that the Carter administration was inclined toward indecision, but that when a decision had to be made it was usually in favor of a weakened U.S. position. That is why Schmidt made so much of a stir in his call for Eurostrategic systems. He understood that U.S.-USSR nuclear parity could neutralize the U.S. deterrent. Schmidt's suspicions of Carter could only have been verified by the neutron bomb debacle of 1978 that seemed to embarrass the chancellor, although it could also be argued that in the face of considerable public opposition to the neutron weapon in West Germany, Carter's decision took Schmidt off the hot seat. Regardless, however, of how one interprets Schmidt's position, there were calls for a "higher measure of continuity and predictability" in U.S. foreign policy. Curiously, many Europeans concentrated only on U.S. "indecision," not on the substance of any decisions reached. That goes a long way in explaining why so many European leaders supported SALT II ratification. The ratification would be a sign of decisiveness, something more important in the eyes of a SPD spokesman Peter Corterier than the fact that SALT II "does not compensate the conceivable vulnerability of the land-based American ICBMs."[22] But it was precisely that vulnerability that led Germans into the gray area of theater nuclear forces in the first place and to the continuing worry over them.

But if U.S. indecision lay at the root of threats to detente, it cannot be assumed that decisive policy action will get the United States off the hook. In a press seminar held in February 1981 in Paris under the sponsorship of the Atlantic Institute for International Affairs, Corterier scored the Reagan administration for a new nationalism "born of the frustrations of various political set-backs." Corterier argued that the United States should not attempt either containment or rearmament (two very decided Reagan policies) but, instead, should concentrate on arms control and East-West cooperation "to make the

USSR a more responsible world power." He went on to complain that "the U.S. has a tendency to rely on the military approach which, though an important adjunct, is a poor substitute for diplomacy."[23]

This kind of switch in standards by a prominent German cannot help but eventually recreate the never-far-from-the-surface cynicism about the Old World that has long been a hallmark of U.S. foreign policy. Some Americans may find it ironic that German politicians should point fingers at the United States for relying too much on military solutions.

The Germans, though, have understandable (if not laudable) reasons for wanting to distance themselves from U.S. assertiveness toward the USSR. Germany's trade relations with the East are an important consideration here, but it can be suspected that even the trade links are an effect, not a cause, of a German orientation toward the East designed to prompt conditions favorable to German reunification. At the present time this is an impractical goal, but often wishes father ideas more effectively than do facts. How else can one account for German beliefs that there are some pro-Western doves in the Politburo or Central Committee, or that it is the United States that pursues an adventurous foreign policy? In Germany, facts notwithstanding, a belief in detente is essential to the dream of reunification.

Some of de Gaulle's notions about U.S.-Soviet relations and his critical comments about U.S. inclination toward adventurism were mentioned earlier. More recently, one finds the French backing off from some of these notions and criticisms, perhaps in a realization of widespread U.S. frustration with, and incomprehension of, allied sniping. Just a few weeks after Corterier's broadside at the United States, French Foreign Minister Jean François-Poncet made the following observations in a speech delivered at Tufts University:

> Europeans have to stop thinking of the United States as the shield behind which they can lay down their burden of responsibilities. They have to stop heaping continuous, contradictory criticism on the United States, complaining one day that it is too weak and the next day that it is overconfident, decrying its presence in other countries but condemning its isolationism, rejecting its involvement yet fearing its disengagement.[24]

These kinds of remarks recognize the frustration felt by many Americans at being held up to a series of double standards. Each country in NATO has specific national goals, but François-Poncet suggested that the United States can no longer be used as a force to make the world safe for either *grandeur* or *Ostpolitik*.

## SOVIET SECURITY AND ECONOMIC CONCERNS

While many in the West and especially in the United States are very apprehensive about the Soviet Union's arms buildup and its expansionist behavior, the Soviet government has its own security concerns. In the East, it sees a hostile Peoples' Republic of China (PRC) with which it shares a long border. In the West, the Communist satellites do not constitute a fully reliable security buffer; the labor strife in Poland, fledgling dissent movements in Czechoslovakia, and the quest of a measure of independence from the Soviet regime displayed again and again by Romania raise questions about the loyalty of some of the Warsaw Treaty Organization (WTO) forces to Moscow. In the South, the Islamic revolution in Iran and the strong opposition of the Arab states and Pakistan to the Afghanistan invasion may evoke anti-Soviet sentiments among the Islamic segments of the USSR population and, thereby, generate perceived or real security risks. If one adds to these vulnerabilities the military power of NATO (which includes a traditionally hostile Turkey), U.S. forces stationed in the Indian Ocean, and the rapprochement between the United States and Japan on the one side and with the PRC on the other, perceptions of capitalist encirclement that Lenin had warned against in the early 1920s are likely to be prominent in the current world image background of most Soviet leaders, and they are apt to have a bearing on Soviet decisions regarding the future of East-West relations.

If, in the minds of the Soviet leadership, the above factors do indeed constitute elements of an encirclement process, the government has responded to the various challenges in different ways. With respect to the PRC, the Soviet Union engaged in border fighting in the late 1960s to bring the territorial disputes to a solution, but it has not initiated a full-scale war, perhaps for fear that it might escalate into a nuclear struggle. On the other hand, in spite of a number of initiatives to start negotiations for ironing out Sino-Soviet differences, no progress has been made in this endeavor. Consequently, it is unlikely that dramatic changes will occur in the foreseeable future; tensions will persist, but actual fighting is improbable,[25] although this may depend on the degree of U.S.-PRC military cooperation.

In response to the pressures for internal liberalization that is evident to varying degrees in all East European countries with the possible exception of Bulgaria and Romania, the Soviet Union has been willing during the last few years to tolerate a limited measure of deviation from the strict Soviet model of a communist state. It has also acquiesced to a degree of foreign policy autonomy in Romania. The Helsinki Accords on European Security and Cooperation may have been partly responsible for the Soviet position. Soviet leaders may be more prone to tolerate gradual and controlled liberalization because it may be less costly in terms of Soviet prestige and appear to be less threatening to the maintenance of Soviet control. But, as Czechoslovakia demonstrated in 1968, Soviet tolerance has its limits. These limits may be determined by geographic and economic factors, and therefore vary from country to country.[26] A definition of Soviet limits may well become apparent when the last word on Soviet behavior toward the Polish labor situation has been written.

As far as the Soviet attitude toward the Islamic problem is concerned, there are no signs that Soviet forces will be withdrawn from Afghanistan. Rather, that country is likely to remain a forward base for the Soviet Union to launch an attack toward the Persian Gulf if a propitious opportunity should present itself or the need for new energy sources should become overwhelming. At a minimum, it appears that the occupation of Afghanistan will serve as a continuing threat and warning to the Gulf states that Soviet intervention as a possible course of action cannot be ignored.

It is difficult to judge at present what the ultimate Soviet response will be toward steep increases in U.S. expenditures for nuclear and conventional weapons, as well as to a strengthened NATO military posture. Although the Soviet Union has traditionally shown great caution in its benefit-cost calculation with respect to embarking on hostilities, misjudgments may occur, especially if threat-of-encirclement perceptions should prevail in the top councils of the Soviet leadership. Under such circumstances, resort to violence vis-à-vis the Atlantic alliance cannot be entirely excluded as a preemptive Soviet course of action. The intensification of U.S.-PRC cooperation in the military field may be a crucial variable.

Economic conditions may play an important role in responses to perceived vulnerabilities of the Soviet Union. With a large amount of Soviet expenditure having been allocated to the production of weapons and the maintenance of very large armed forces (11 to 13 percent of GNP), the civilian economy has suffered and the consumer has been neglected. Lagging productivity and poor management have hampered the output of consumer goods, while inefficiencies in the production of agricultural commodities have necessitated the extensive importation of grain.

It is interesting to note that the economies of some of the East European satellites are performing more efficiently and are more advanced in terms of GNP per capita and living standards provided than has been possible in the USSR.[27] Although the acquisition of needed technologies for the more effective production of consumer goods has aided in ameliorating the availability of such goods, it remains insufficient to meet the demands of the Soviet populace and has not improved living standards. It would be pleasant to think that this situation provides leverage for the West to change Soviet behavior along lines satisfying the objectives of the Atlantic alliance by withholding needed technologies. But it is doubtful that a militarily powerful regime such as the Soviet Union would agree to such a trade-off. Indeed, such action would be perceived as acknowledging the Soviet Union's economic weakness before the world and would seriously undermine the regime's legitimacy. It seems more plausible that the poor economic performance of the USSR in the consumer field coupled with perceptions of encirclement might provide incentives for the Soviet leadership to undertake a nuclear first strike against the West which, if successful in eliminating the U.S. ability for a counterstrike, would solve the problems of encirclement and the economy. Western Europe under Soviet control could be forced to furnish all the technologies and financial resources the USSR would require for a complete domination of the world. The authors do not predict such a course of events; indeed, they do not view it as likely, yet it is a possibility, however remote, that cannot be ignored entirely.

**THE IMPACT OF PUBLIC OPINION**

As stated earlier, a major part of this volume analyzes public opinion data in selected NATO countries that are relevant to Atlantic defense within the context of East-West relations and may have a bearing on the perceptions of NATO policymakers. It is always risky to speculate on the extent of the influence that public opinion may have on the perceptions of those who participate in foreign policy and security decisionmaking, and it is equally difficult to pinpoint the linkage and perhaps causality between perceptions and actual decisions.

There is considerable argument among political scientists about under what conditions public opinion influences the formulation of foreign policy and what the extent of this influence is. It is generally agreed that, on highly emotional issues such as the Vietnam war, public opinion can have an enormous impact on policy formulation and implementation. For better or worse, it was the increasingly negative view of that war by the American public that forced the hands of President Nixon and Secretary of State Henry Kissinger to seek an end to the Vietnam involvement. In less controversial and less emotional situations, public opinion may impose some broad constraints or parameters on foreign policymakers, it may "permit" them to formulate certain policies, but it generally does not force their hands to engage in specific policies.[28] In many instances of foreign policymaking, regardless of whether "high" or "low" politics is involved, public opinion plays a distinctly minor part because the general public is either not interested or is poorly informed regarding the issues at stake.

Public opinion, of course, can also be and has been shaped (or manipulated) by the policymakers. John Foster Dulles, secretary of state during the Eisenhower administration, declared once: "A Secretary of State who waits for public opinion of the right kind to develop before taking action is derelict in his duty." Yet Dulles also believed that no administration would move too far ahead of public sentiment, and that officials should not neglect to inform the public at frequent intervals to "bring it along" in support of needed policies.[29] Clearly, the molding of public opinion in foreign affairs has been attempted since Franklin D. Roosevelt's tenure in the White House by various means, ranging from "fireside chats" to intensive news coverage of foreign trips undertaken by the president and his chief foreign policymakers.

Undoubtedly, this management of news has successfully shaped public opinion in many instances.

The security and economic problems faced by the NATO countries in the 1980s are of a magnitude that should make it imperative for policymakers to listen carefully to the voices of the people. These voices may well be different in individual countries of the alliance. Much depends on the accuracy of the perceptions held by the public, and this, in turn, depends on the mix of cognitive and affective factors that condition public opinion. For example, public opinion in Western Europe on East-West relations may be more influenced by trade and employment figures affecting their country, while U.S. opinions cannot be divorced from fear of communism which, with the exception of the World War II alliance with the Soviet Union, has pervaded U.S. attitudes since 1933.[30] Nevertheless, although perception backgrounds and sources in different NATO countries are at variance, whatever public opinion expresses on Atlantic defense, NATO, and East-West relations constitutes the political reality that must be taken into account by policymakers in all NATO countries and should be a guide for their decisionmaking. Indeed, they would run a serious risk in terms of policy intent and actual policy outcome if public opinion within the alliance were to be ignored. This study hopes to make a contribution to alliance policymaking by presenting a comparative analysis and assessment of relevant public opinion, primarily in the United States, West Germany, Great Britain, and France.

Even if the perceptions of policymakers were to be influenced by expression of public opinion, these perceptions may not have a concrete input into actual decisions on Atlantic defense issues. As Robert Jervis has noted, it is most difficult to explain decisions because of the multitude of variables that need to be considered. A decisionmaker's images of the world, belief systems, experiences in the past, perceptions of both the adversaries' intentions and the international situation (perhaps different from "objective" reality), bureaucratic constraints and incentives, and domestic political determinants all play a role in decisions relating to Atlantic defense and East-West relations.[31] Public opinion is obviously a domestic determinant and, since this study deals with a number of countries, inferences drawn from survey results in one country by the policymakers of that country may differ from those drawn by policymakers in an allied country. It is reasonable to assume that public opinion in the policymaker's own country has a greater impact on that individual's decisionmaking process than on policymakers in another country. As a consequence, different expressions of public opinion on issue areas in the NATO countries may become sources of misunderstanding and friction among the NATO allies. This brings up again the question of the accuracy and competency of the perceptions held by the public, since decisionmakers in different NATO countries may consider this an important factor when drawing their inferences from public opinion polls.

This analysis of public opinion will begin by examining the image of NATO in the United States, which will be followed by an evaluation of U.S. attitudes regarding defense in general and NATO in particular (Chapters 2 to 4). Chapter 5 will focus mainly on the views of the public in West Germany, France, and Britain. The final part of the book will offer conclusions on the potential impact of public opinion on defense-related decisions within the NATO alliance and speculation on these findings that may affect the future of the Atlantic defense.

**NOTES**

1. V. D. Sokolovskiy, *Military Strategy*, 3d ed., trans. Harriet East Scott (New York: Crane, Russak, 1975).
2. George Rathjens and Jack Ruina, "Nuclear Doctrine and Rationality," *Daedalus* 110 (Winter 1981): 179-87.
3. F. William Scott, *Soviet Sources of Military Doctrine* (New York: Crane, Russak, 1975).
4. Charles de Gaulle, *Major Addresses, Statements and Press Conferences of General Charles de Gaulle: May 19, 1958-January 31, 1964* (New York: French Embassy, Press and Information Division, 1964), p. 218.
5. U.S. Congress, Senate, Committee on Foreign Relations, *U.S.-U.S.S.R. Strategic Policies*, 93d Cong., 2d sess., 1974.
6. Edward Luttwak, *Strategy and Politics* (New Brunswick and London: Trans-Action, 1980), p. 51.
7. Walter Goldstein, "Calculating Defense," in *Defense Politics of the Atlantic Alliance*, ed. Edwin H. Fedder (New York: Praeger, 1980), pp. 131-52, esp. p. 142.
8. Colin S. Gray, "Action and Reaction in the Nuclear Arms Race," *Military Review* 51 (August 1971): 16-26; and Graham T. Allison and Frederick A. Morris, "Armaments and Arms Control: Exploring the Determinants of Military Weapons," *Daedalus* 104 (Summer 1975): 99-129.
9. Kevin N. Lewis, "Intermediate-Range Nuclear Weapons," *Scientific American* 243 (December 1980): 63-73, on p. 64.
10. Ibid., p. 73.
11. Ibid.
12. George Custance, "Is the XM1 Tank Obsolete?" *National Defense* 65 (October 1980): 60-62, on p. 62.
13. Leon Gouré, William G. Hyland, and Colin S. Gray, *The Emerging Strategic Environment: Implications for Ballistic Missile Defense* (Cambridge: Institute for Foreign Policy Analysis, 1979), p. 27.
14. Robert S. Jordan, ed., *Europe and the Superpowers* (Boston: Allyn & Bacon, 1971), p. 35.
15. Charles de Gaulle, *Major Addresses, Statements and Press Conferences: March 17, 1964-May 16, 1967* (New York: French Embassy Press and Information Service, 1967), p. 118.
16. U.S. Congress, Senate, Committee on Foreign Relations, *SALT and the NATO Allies*, 96th Cong., 1st sess., 1979, pp. 54-57.
17. Ibid., pp. 41-44.
18. U.S. Congress, Senate, Committee on Foreign Relations, *NATO—A Status Report*, 96th Cong., 2d sess., 1980, p. 6.

19. See also Chancellor Schmidt's address to the Bundestag, April 9, 1981, on safeguarding peace in Europe; German Information Service, *Relay from Bonn*, April 10, 1981.

20. *SALT and the NATO Allies*, p. 10.

21. Quoted in William G. Hyland, "The Atlantic Crisis," *Daedalus* 110 (Winter 1981): 45.

22. *SALT and the NATO Allies*, p. 45.

23. "What Can President Reagan and the Europeans Expect from One Another?" Press Seminar summary released by the Atlantic Institute for International Affairs, Paris, February 4, 1981, p. 2.

24. The quotation is taken from a transcript of François-Poncet's speech printed by the French Embassy's Press and Information Service, p. 1.

25. See U.S. Congress, Senate, Committee on Foreign Relations, *Perceptions: Relations between the United States and the Soviet Union* (n.d.), pp. 119-224.

26. For details see ibid., pp. 153-70.

27. Ibid., p. 172.

28. See William R. Caspari, "The Mood Theory: A Showing of Public Opinion and Foreign Policy," *American Political Science Review* 64 (June 1970): 536-47. See also the seminal study by Gabriel Almond, *The American People and Foreign Policy*, rev. ed. (New York: Praeger, 1960); and Thomas A. Bailey, *Man in the Street* (New York: Macmillan, 1948).

29. Quotation in Cecil V. Crabb, Jr., *American Foreign Policy in the Nuclear Age*, 3d ed. (New York: Harper & Row, 1972), p. 170.

30. For greater details on this problem, see the contribution by Carl Marcey in *Perception: Relations between the United States and the Soviet Union*, pp. 311-16.

31. *Perceptions and Misperceptions in International Politics* (Princeton, N.J.: Princeton University Press, 1976).

# 2

# THE PUBLIC IMAGE OF NATO IN THE UNITED STATES

**PRINT MEDIA AND TELEVISION**

To appreciate fully the perceptions of the American people regarding NATO and the Atlantic defense and their possible impact on U.S. foreign and security policies, it is important to examine these perceptions against the image of NATO held by the public. The formation of this image has been influenced by various factors such as historical experiences, individual belief systems, and personal values; but the most significant factor may be the views presented by different news media over a period of time. Since for U.S. foreign policymakers, regardless of their political persuasions, NATO has always been a crucial instrument for the assurance of American security, a favorable image of NATO in both the United States and in other NATO member states has been regarded as extremely important. Similar considerations have prevailed in most other NATO countries that look to NATO as the best guarantee for their territorial integrity and peace. Hence, for NATO's Information Service, the most crucial task has been and continues to be the pursuit of an effective public information policy. This, in turn, raises a number of questions:

- What are NATO's major public information goals?
- Which means are used to attain these goals?
- Which channels (pipelines) are used to make these means effective in presenting the desired image of NATO and how well do these pipelines function?
- What is the final product presented by the various media in terms of the NATO image projected?

This chapter focuses mainly on an analysis of seven newspapers (*New York Times, Chicago Tribune, Detroit News, Los Angeles Times, San Francisco Chronicle, Houston Post,* and *New Orleans Times-Picayune;* three weekly newsmagazines (*Time, Newsweek,* and *U.S. News and World Report*); and CBS. ABC and NBC were omitted because the records of their documentaries are only on videotape (stored at the TV News Archives at Vanderbilt University in Nashville, Tennessee), and can be viewed only with a videotape player. Popular economic and scientific periodicals such as *Business Week* and *Scientific American* were also perused. Finally, the impact of *NATO Review* and the *Atlantic Community Quarterly* is briefly assessed. Nongovernmental organizations (such as the Atlantic Council of the United States) and academic conferences on transatlantic or NATO problems were not covered because their impact on the public image of NATO is generally small, although some elite opinions may be affected.

At first this study was confined to covering the years 1977 and 1978. However, in view of the thirtieth anniversary of NATO in 1979, the authors felt it would be useful to evaluate the effects of the undoubtedly stepped-up NATO public information efforts during that year on the NATO image in the United States and to compare it with the preceding two years.

This chapter conveys the impression of the effects that resulted from two major NATO image-producing activities: coverage by seven selected newspapers from 1977 to 1978 (plus three months in 1979) and by CBS News. In addition, two comparative in-depth analyses for one critical month—April 1978—were undertaken by spotlighting coverage of CBS News and the *New York Times* of an important transatlantic controversy, the possible construction and deployment in Europe of the neutron bomb.

## PUBLIC INFORMATION

In conversations with David Kyd when he was NATO spokesman, the following public information goals and emphases were identified:

- NATO remains a very important factor for the security of all alliance members.
- NATO is a significant tool for political consultation among member states, and this role must be stressed more.
- NATO plays a pivotal role in safeguarding the democratic way of life and the democratic values of the alliance members, and this mission must receive increased prominence.
- NATO's participation in and sponsorship of studies regarding the challenges of modern society need to be brought to the attention of the public.

The main instrument for the dissemination of information by NATO headquarters is the press briefing. No transcripts are available and no record seems to be kept. Press releases play a minor part; indeed, only 42 releases were issued from January 1, 1977 to December 31, 1978. Some of these were communiqués following important NATO meetings; others provided background information and analyses. In addition, NATO films, the *NATO Review*, and NATO handbooks are important vehicles for the dissemination of pertinent information. An Information and Cultural Committee assists in the coordination of public information activities.

**PIPELINES INPUT AND OUTPUT**

The different pieces of information offered by the NATO Press Service travel through a variety of pipelines and channels to the user news organizations. Moreover, other official and unofficial sources, including the NATO member governments, private research organizations, and individuals working for NATO or the diplomatic missions to NATO, are utilized for NATO news coverage.

None of the media surveyed in this study has a government correspondent assigned to NATO. The *New York Times* employs its defense and security authority, Drew Middleton, as a supervisor over NATO-related news stories; apparently Middleton had a close relationship with NATO's former top military commander, General Alexander Haig. For the coverage of major stories, the *New York Times* uses its permanent correspondents in Paris and Bonn and, for the remainder—often very specialized news—it employs stringers (free-lance journalists working for several newspapers) located in Brussels.

The *Chicago Tribune* has sent U.S.-based reporters to Brussels for special events such as NATO maneuvers, but generally seems to rely more on the news wire services such as Associated Press (AP) and United Press International (UPI). Permanent correspondents in one of Europe's capitals may also be used for major stories from time to time.

The *Los Angeles Times* has its own wire service and falls back on AP, UPI, and Reuters when needed. For the *New Orleans Times-Picayune*, the AP and the *Los Angeles Times-Washington Post* wire services are the most important sources of NATO news. The AP is preferred over other wire services for spot news, and the *Los Angeles Times-Washington Post* service is used for analytical stories.

The *Detroit News* uses mainly wire services for its NATO spot news, with the *Los Angeles Times-Washington Post* and the *New York Times* services given preference over AP and UPI. On occasion, stringers are also employed. The *San Francisco Chronicle* seems to have similar preferences for the use of the wire services for NATO stories, but also makes use of Reuters. Editorials on NATO are prepared by the editorial board, which communicates them to the spot news staff but does not consult the latter regarding the contents.

The *Houston Post* employs the AP, UPI, and the Knight-Ridder newspapers service for NATO stories, but also makes use of an in-house analyst who has a military background. Analyses by *The Economist* and the *Christian Science Monitor* may also be utilized. Stringers are rarely sources for stories. Editorials come from the editorial staff, with apparently little communication with the spot news people. The opening of a London bureau for European news has been considered.

The newsmagazines generally utilize their permanent correspondents in Europe to cover NATO, but may fall back on the wire services occasionally. The major television networks employ their own camera crews and reporters on major NATO stories, but for spot news may utilize the wire services.

The wire services obviously play an important role in the transmission of NATO news. Their specialists on NATO and bureau chiefs in Brussels act as the first gatekeepers on pipeline information inputs, and choose which story and what sources to use. For the story to make it to the United States depends very much on the quality and expertise of the specialist monitoring NATO affairs and his or her major sources.

Once a story has been cleared by the bureau chief for transmission to headquarters in New York, it is up to the foreign news editor of the particular wire service whether to transmit it further to subscribers or to kill it. Eighty to ninety percent of the stories move on, although some rewriting may take place. The final gatekeeper is the foreign news editor of the subscribing newspaper or television news network. Space or time considerations then become salient, as well as the general interest of readers of a particular newspaper in foreign news. According to an AP senior management official, in-depth stories or analyses have a better chance of acceptance than straight news or spot news. The acceptance rate of the former may average 50 percent, while the latter might be about 30 percent. Thus what goes into the pipelines in Brussels may be quite different in quantity and thrust when it is seen or heard as "news" by readers and listeners in the United States. Moreover, it is important to keep in mind that editorials do not usually originate with the foreign news desk, but with the editorial department. Hence, the composite public image of NATO flows from several distinct groups of people. This may lead to difficulties in image analysis and evaluation.

## NATO COVERAGE OF SEVEN NEWSPAPERS

### Spot News

Between January 1, 1977 and December 1978, the *New York Times* carried 411 NATO stories, nearly half of the combined total of all the newspapers examined. Its share would have been even higher if the paper had not been strike-bound for well over two months. The lowest scores for the two-year period were recorded by the *San Francisco Chronicle*, the *Times-Picayune*, and the *Detroit News* (see Table 2.1). These newspapers have primarily a strong regional orientation inclining them to local and national news. The relatively low score of the *Los Angeles Times*, one of the most prominent and respected papers in the United States, is astonishing. The reason may well be the long distance from Europe and its major concern with Pacific affairs. This may also explain that the lowest score of all newspapers is that of the *San Francisco Chronicle*.

There is no correlation between the number of press releases issued by NATO and the number of stories published on NATO, except during the months of the biannual ministerial meetings in May and December. The larger number of NATO stories in the *Chicago Tribune* in April and May of 1978 may well be due to the presence at NATO headquarters and other NATO installations of two of its reporters. Despite detailed news releases on this score, there also appears to be little response to the pursuit of some of NATO's public information objectives, such as the hoped-for recognition of NATO's involvement in the efforts to find solutions to the challenges of modern society. Even NATO's political consultation function per se finds little echo in the U.S. news media researched.

**Editorials**

Most news accounts during the period under review showed basic sympathy with NATO defense efforts. NATO is regarded as an essential part of U.S. security. However, in the editorials, frequent criticism was expressed when NATO was seen in the broad perspective of an extensive and necessary alliance. In the 11 editorials appearing in the *New York Times* during this period, 3 were definitely critical. One of these suggested that not enough was being done to "rationalize" the cooperative effort of NATO (June 17, 1978). Another criticized Carter's handling of the neutron bomb issue, which resulted in making NATO appear weak, to be giving in to Soviet pressures and, thereby, leaving some of the allies out on a limb (April 6, 1978). The last critical editorial touched on NATO only peripherally and chided the United States for not clearly defining its goals regarding the SALT talks.

The *Chicago Tribune's* 14 editorials on NATO during the period under review were more often critical than favorable (8 out of 14). Two of these editorials criticized the handling of the neutron bomb within the context of NATO (April 6 and 15, 1978). One editorial wondered why the Europeans wanted the cruise missile but not the neutron bomb, and called for European cooperation in the production of the missile (November 12, 1977). Two editorials considered NATO to be lagging behind the Warsaw Pact in military capabilities (January 29 and May 13, 1977). Another editorial thought NATO could not stop a Soviet attack; sending an additional 8,000 U.S. soldiers was too little (January 13, 1978). Two editorials expressed concern about the Greek-Turkish dispute and supported lifting the arms embargo against Turkey (May 14 and June 18, 1978).

Of the ten editorials in the *Los Angeles Times* during the period, four were critical. One complained about attempts to sabotage weapons standardization (especially with respect to tanks) that was needed to make NATO cost-effective (March 17, 1977). Another expressed concern about an overreliance on nuclear weapons that is brought about by an increased Soviet buildup of both nuclear and conventional forces. NATO, therefore, should increase conventional forces (May 12, 1977). The third editorial criticized Europeans for delays in openly supporting the neutron bomb. However, it argued that the United States should not deploy this bomb until a clear European consensus exists for it (October 13, 1977). The fourth editorial urged the European allies not to find excuses for not increasing their defense spending and follow the United States' lead in this matter (December 27, 1978).

Three of the four editorials in the *New Orleans Times-Picayune* were critical. One believed that the delay in building the neutron bomb would decrease NATO's defensive capabilities and may force the Soviets to build their own neutron bomb first (April 26, 1978). The second urged the lifting of the arms embargo against Turkey and asked Carter to use his energy to solve the Cyprus dispute, arguing that both actions, in the long run, would strengthen NATO (June 1, 1978). A similar stand was taken in the editorial of December 1, 1978.

Two of the three editorials on NATO published by the *Detroit News* dealt with weapons procurement. They supported the idea of weapon standardization and showed understanding that the European allies want to increase their share of the weapons production. However, the Europeans must also accept adverse production decisions with grace when, for example, Chrysler won the contract on the new NATO tank (March 12 and 13, 1977). In a third editorial during the period under review, fears were raised about Eurocommunism threatening NATO in the event communists entered either the Italian or French government, although it was acknowledged that the United States has an obligation not to interfere in the politics of either country (January 18, 1978). Thus all three editorials showed apprehension and were somewhat critical.

Of the four editorials in the *San Francisco Chronicle*, one complained about the lack of security stemming from thousands of East German spies in the Federal Republic endangering NATO secrets, and suggested the need for stronger security measures in West Germany (December 15, 1977). Another editorial took the U.S. government to task for not being able to repeal the congressional ban on weapons sales to Turkey (June 6, 1978), a problem that

**TABLE 2.1: Monthly Totals of NATO Newspaper Stories**

|  | New York Times | Chicago Tribune | N.O. Times-Picayune | L.A. Times | Detroit News | Houston Post | San Francisco Chronicle |
|---|---|---|---|---|---|---|---|
| *1977* | | | | | | | |
| January | 14 | 7 | 4 | 4 | 2 | 6 | 3 |
| February | 16 | 2 | 2 | 1 | 1 | 2 | — |
| March | 16 | 2 | 1 | 1 | 4 | — | 1 |
| April | 18 | — | — | 3 | 2 | 2 | — |
| May | 22 | 7 | 3 | 7 | 5 | 14 | 4 |
| June | 13 | — | — | 3 | — | — | — |
| July | 12 | 4 | 1 | 2 | 5 | 2 | 2 |
| August | 10 | 3 | 4 | 2 | 2 | 1 | 2 |
| September | 12 | 4 | 1 | 1 | 4 | 2 | 2 |
| October | 15 | 2 | 3 | 3 | 4 | 3 | 2 |
| November | 10 | 5 | — | 2 | 3 | 2 | 1 |
| December | 26 | 7 | 2 | 10 | 2 | 7 | 7 |
| Subtotals | 184 | 43 | 21 | 39 | 34 | 41 | 22 |

## 1978

| Month | | | | | | | |
|---|---|---|---|---|---|---|---|
| January | 24 | 5 | 1 | 3 | 5 | 3 | 5 |
| February | 20 | 6 | 2 | 2 | 2 | 4 | 1 |
| March | 13 | 4 | 2 | 3 | 2 | 3 | 1 |
| April | 62 | 14 | 4 | 2 | 3 | 7 | 3 |
| May | 34 | 12 | 5 | 8 | 6 | 8 | 3 |
| June | 26 | 7 | 10 | 8 | 1 | 10 | 9 |
| July | 9 | 2 | 3 | — | — | 5 | 5 |
| August | on strike | 1 | — | 1 | 1 | 1 | 2 |
| September | on strike | 6 | 4 | 4 | 3 | 3 | 2 |
| October | 10 | 6 | 1 | 3 | 3 | 4 | 1 |
| November | 10 | 1 | 3 | 6 | 3 | 3 | 1 |
| December | 19 | 5 | 8 | 9 | 5 | 5 | 6 |
| Subtotals | 227 | 69 | 43 | 49 | 34 | 56 | 39 |
| Grand totals | 411 | 112 | 64 | 88 | 68 | 97 | 61 |

1977 Aggregate Total: 384
1978 Aggregate Total: 517
Final Total: 901

has since been solved. A third editorial praised NATO's efforts in increasing its military capability and did not consider it paradoxical that, at the same time, the United States wanted to come to an agreement with the Soviet Union for a mutual and balanced reduction of weapons (May 12, 1978). Finally, an editorial challenged the platitudes of a December 1978 NATO communiqué that left unmentioned challenges by Romania's President Nicolae Ceauscescu to the Kremlin's demands for increased military spending by the Warsaw Pact allies, an event that seemed to offer opportunities for a "political dialogue" between NATO and the Pact countries (December 11, 1978).

The *Houston Post* published a surprisingly large number of editorials during 1977 and 1978 on NATO (ten) and an above-average number of news analyses. Two reasons may account for this interest in NATO: Houston considers itself an international city, perhaps the oil capital of the United States; and the presence of the military analyst among its staff may focus greater interest on strategic affairs. The subjects of the editorials covered many of the topics found in the other papers examined: the new U.S. weapons, such as the neutron bomb and the cruise missiles (December 16, 1977 and April 1978); the NATO-Warsaw Pact relationship (December 20, 1977 and June 7, 1978); Turkish-Greek relations (April 16 and June 9, 1978); Spain's membership in NATO, which it advocated (January 15, 1977 and June 5, 1978); and support for greater NATO and U.S. defense spending, which, according to the editor, was urgently needed (May 19, 1977 and September 19, 1978). Generally, all editorials fell into the category of constructive criticism.

While some of these editorials have been labeled as "critical," it should be stressed that none questioned the need for a strong, effective NATO. Indeed, the thrust of these editorials was to urge needed improvement to further strengthen the alliance. This is especially obvious in the complaints about lagging standardization of weapons, the lack of harmony between Greece and Turkey, and the problem of consensus on the production and employment of the neutron bomb. However, these problems often defy "rational" solutions because domestic political considerations in the NATO member states have, at times, become paramount, requiring the satisfaction of demands made by influential home constituencies. While, as a consequence, negative factors are injected into NATO's public image in the United States, they do not affect the basic support shown elsewhere by the seven newspapers or diminish the generally positive picture of NATO conveyed to their readership.

### NATO's Thirty-Year Anniversary

Since there are no data on the *Detroit News, Houston Post*, and *San Francisco Chronicle* for the first six months of 1979, the comparison with the 1977 and 1978 figures on NATO news stories for the anniversary period has to be limited to the other four papers.

Surprisingly, the number of NATO stories during March-May 1979, the period including the NATO anniversary, was on balance smaller than in 1977 and 1978. This is especially noticeable in the case of the *New York Times* (see Table 2.2). The reason for this situation is the neutron bomb controversy in spring 1978 that produced many stories bearing on NATO. Another reason may be that anniversaries are not really "news" and that, for most Americans, NATO is seen as a necessary and fully accepted organization. Even the three editorials appearing in the four newspapers surveyed do not touch on the anniversary issue, but on substantive problems (see *New York Times*, March 1 and May 22, 1979; and *Los Angeles Times*, April 20, 1979).

## NATO COVERAGE BY NEWSMAGAZINES

Of the five newsmagazines selected for closer examination regarding NATO coverage, three are general interest publications—*Time, Newsweek,* and *U.S. News and World Report*—while the two others focus on special interests—

**TABLE 2.2: Comparison of Publication of NATO-Related Articles**

|  | March | April | May | Total |
| --- | --- | --- | --- | --- |
| New York Times | | | | |
| 1979 | 12 | 8 | 17 | 37 |
| 1978 | 13 | 62 | 34 | 109 |
| 1977 | 16 | 18 | 22 | 56 |
| Chicago Tribune | | | | |
| 1979 | 4 | 7 | 2 | 13 |
| 1978 | 4 | 14 | 12 | 30 |
| 1977 | 2 | 0 | 7 | 9 |
| New Orleans Times-Picayune | | | | |
| 1979 | 1 | 4 | 0 | 5 |
| 1978 | 1 | 4 | 5 | 11 |
| 1977 | 1 | 0 | 3 | 4 |
| Los Angeles Times | | | | |
| 1979 | 4 | 4 | 0 | 8 |
| 1978 | 3 | 2 | 8 | 13 |
| 1977 | 1 | 3 | 7 | 11 |

*Business Week* and *Scientific American*. Table 2.3 shows that for the period under consideration, *Newsweek* and *Business Week* carried more NATO stories than the other magazines. Further analysis indicates that the stories of these two publications were concentrated in the first half of 1978; none of the stories in 1979 dealt with NATO's thirtieth anniversary.

The tenor of all stories in the newsmagazines suggests basic NATO support, but also criticism about weaknesses in NATO policies and the behavior of the NATO allies. The furor over the neutron bomb was discussed in several stories (for example, two stories in *Newsweek*, April 7, 1978, pp. 34-40; and *Scientific American*, May 1978). The problem of increased NATO spending was examined critically by *Business Week* (June 5 and October 23, 1978) and *Scientific American* (October 1978). The Soviet Union's military and political undercutting of NATO was deplored on several occasions (*Time*, June 27, 1977 and June 12, 1978; *U.S. News and World Report*, January 17, 1977 and June 12, 1978; and *Business Week*, February 27 and March 27, 1978), and the spy problem was examined in *Newsweek* (March 19, 1979). Finally, the U.S. embargo on Turkey was discussed in *Business Week* (April 3, 1978). All these and other newsmagazine stories are in-depth analyses and urge remedies for the perceived vulnerabilities.

### NATO-Related Publications

A brief content analysis of the *NATO Review*, published six times a year by the NATO Information Service, suggests a serious, high-level approach to the examination of possible solutions to various problems plaguing the alliance. The authors expressing their opinions in the *Review* are mostly military and civilian officials of NATO and the member governments of that organization, parliamentarians of the allies with special expertise in strategic and international affairs, and academicians with similar interests. While the *NATO Review* is a valuable contribution to the scholarly discussion of the many difficult features of this extraordinary and complex intergovernmental organi-

**TABLE 2.3: NATO Coverage by Major Newsmagazines**

|  | 1977 | 1978 | March-May 1979 | Total |
|---|---|---|---|---|
| Time | 2 | 1 | 0 | 3 |
| Newsweek | 2 | 7 | 2 | 11 |
| U.S. News and World Report | 2 | 2 | 1 | 5 |
| Business Week | 1 | 5 | 1 | 7 |
| Scientific American | 2 | 3 | 0 | 5 |

zation, and while the U.S. Department of State makes a valiant effort to promote the distribution of this publication, its impact on the NATO image in the United States is likely to be minor. Many recipients of the *Review* might somehow suspect its "pro-domo" thrust, and other simply will not find the time to read still another publication.

A greater impact, at least on the elite segment of U.S. public opinion, may be produced by the *Atlantic Community Quarterly*, published by the Atlantic Council of the United States, Inc. The majority of articles found in this periodical are reprints of essays, lectures, and declarations that have appeared elsewhere or were given in a variety of forums. Few original essays find their way into the *Quarterly*. A major criterion for selection of articles is relevance for the Atlantic community and, indirectly, NATO. The material presented in the *Quarterly* is consistently of high quality and is usually supportive of overall NATO goals.

## NATO IN APRIL 1978:
## A COMPARATIVE ANALYSIS OF TWO U.S. MEDIA

Any appraisal of the image of the alliance in the U.S. media requires solid evidence, but the available evidence is rather like a forest in that one can take a long view and see the forest as a whole, or one can take a short view and see the trees. The real difficulty lies in trying to find out what view the public takes: are they forest watchers or tree watchers? Answering this question might be made easier by taking a retrospective look at the trees and then the forest. In doing so, the authors have selected an unusually rugged set of terrain, so to speak. It was in April 1978 that President Carter announced his decision on U.S. production of the neutron warhead, or the so-called N-bomb. Carter's decision was a difficult one to make and attracted intense media coverage. It also attracted coverage of NATO since the weapon was specifically designed as a counterforce to Warsaw Pact tank supremacy. All in all, this decision—a decision to delay a final decision—created an atypical media month. But images are largely forged by atypical events—events that leave an imprint.

NATO's media month of April 1978 began in the *New York Times* of April 1 with a page 5 comment chiding Carter's delay in producing the neutron bomb, and discussion of European unhappiness with Carter's foreign policy style. Thus, on April 1, the content of the *New York Times* was weapon and personality oriented, as far as NATO-related news was concerned. On the second and third of the month, however, interest turned to the vexing threats and counterthreats coming from Turkey and Greece over the U.S. arms embargo to Turkey stemming from the Cyprus invasion. This was weekend news, but unpleasant at that.

Then, on April 4, the *New York Times* announced Carter's intention to cancel neutron weapon production and discussed the complicated implications for NATO. This announcement by the *New York Times* elicited considerable comment by other media, both press and electronic. From this point it is instructive to see how the *New York Times* and CBS News treated NATO stories for the month. Table 2.4 shows a calendar of events that takes the flow of news in the two sources tree by tree. This calendar is not fully fair to either medium. The *New York Times* stories reported are greatly abbreviated, while the CBS stories are summarized only on the basis of scripts—the tone of correspondents' voices and the impact of live and filmed (including taped) visual material are impossible to convey here. Still, the summaries are a useful tool for making a point of departure.

First, the *New York Times* had the opportunity to make a much greater volume of information available; volume is clearly a newspaper's forte. CBS had the opportunity to display television's strong point—visual impact—with clips of tanks rolling across the north European plain. It is commonplace to observe the television offers immediacy, while newspapers offer depth. But in the case of the neutron weapon, the contrast between depth and immediacy was not stunning. There are two reasons for this: it is hard to find an indepth treatment of a secrecy-shrouded weapon, based upon the behavior of isotopes subjected to nuclear fission, in a mass-circulation daily; and secondhand reports of diplomatic tete-a-tetes over weapons acquisition just do not have the kind of immediacy at which television is best. Rather, CBS's reports were highly mediated. Thus the basic story of the neutron weapon came across rather similarly in the two media. It appeared as an antitank weapon of a controversial nature that ended up embarrassing Carter and endangering the political career of Chancellor Schmidt.

But there is a second point to be made if one looks at volume in another way, a way that encompasses more than just the neutron weapon. If this is done, one sees a more delineated separation of the two sources of news. To return to the forest/trees analogy, the *New York Times* had a more variegated set of trees. CBS confined its NATO-related news of April 1978 to virtually nothing but the neutron weapon. The *New York Times*, on the other hand, developed a continuing subplot: the Greek-Turkish conflict over Cyprus. This was not a "breaking" story, so to speak, but a set of annotations to a confrontation of cultures first chronicled in the *Illiad*. It is tempting to suggest that the *New York Times*, then, put the neutron weapon in a broader strategic context. While readers had a chance to see a wider context by referring to the *New York Times*, there is no evidence from this particular month that they would have been motivated to do so by this newspaper. The additional information was there, but not emphasized. Instead, it may have been smothered by the drama of the neutron weapon.

There is a third point to be made about the individual stories, in addition to the greater number and variety of *New York Times* stories: continuity. After

April 10, 1978, CBS coverage of NATO-related items dropped to virtually nothing: a short notice was given to a relaxation of Soviet objections to the sharing of cruise missile technology with NATO, and a French denial of having exploded a neutron weapon. On the other hand, the *New York Times* continued to cover NATO, and sometimes ran several stories per day.

Consequently, this look at NATO's image for a single month, concentrating on stories in isolation, makes it clear that a newspaper can cover a greater number and variety of stories if it chooses to do so, over a longer period of time. In terms of the neutron bomb alone though, it is not really supportable to argue that there was greater depth in the printed media's presentation. Either the *New York Times* or CBS could have given an attentive follower a fairly accurate idea of what was happening and what the major parties to the issue felt and said. The neutron weapon controversy was a crisis, however, and it is encouraging to note that in this particular crisis there was some redundancy to the U.S. communications system.

Having said that, one should step back a bit from the individual stories and try to look at the ensemble. Figures 2.1, 2.2, and 2.3 display the frequency of coverage for the entire month—they are a visualization of the calendar or log set forth in Table 2.4. They capture well the points about volume and continuity, but not the point of variety. Still, they help to raise the question skirted so far in this volume: the meaning to the image of NATO of the coverage discussed here. Separating meaning and volume can be done only in an artificial sense, since the volume of coverage itself has meaning. Yet, for analytical purposes, it is convenient here to concentrate on content specifically.

One way the reader can approach this is by reading the log for the *New York Times* all at once, and then the log for CBS—the order is a matter of indifference. What Table 2.4 suggests, appropriately so, is that the NATO of the *New York Times* is a fractious aggregate of nations beset in the northern tier by an armored enemy, and in the southern tier by ethnic rivalries. It appears to be dependent upon U.S. hegemony, a hegemony based upon weapons technology and a leadership style best called "distracted." Curiously, small nations in the alliance—Greece, Turkey, and the Netherlands—seem to have a lot of influence, an ability to paralyze their larger neighbors and allies. In the CBS material, NATO comes across more as people and less as an institution—Carter, Vance, assorted congressmen, and an occasional German are the essence of NATO. Historians might be impressed with the argument that the *New York Times*'s coverage was very Toynbeesque—a tale of the clashes of civilizations—while CBS's coverage was more in the "great men" school.

Both images are meritorious and hardly mutually exclusive, since both media do convey a common kind of image of NATO: a weapons-oriented collectivity with a rather open decisionmaking process, with plenty of room for smaller individuals and groups to be heard. Despite U.S. hegemony, there is no suggestion that Germans, Dutch, Turks, or Greeks are satellites of the United States. In that respect, one element that does emerge from both media

**TABLE 2.4: Calendar of News Events Covered by New York Times and CBS News, April 1978**

| New York Times | April 1978 | CBS News |
|---|---|---|
| European criticisms of Carter's foreign policy style. | Saturday, 1 | |
| Criticism of Carter's delay in producing neutron weapons. | Sunday, 2 | |
| Turks threaten to withdraw from NATO if arms embargo is not lifted. | Monday, 3 | |
| Greece warns U.S. it will not rejoin the military arm of NATO if Turkish embargo is lifted. | | |
| Carter cancels neutron bomb. | Tuesday, 4 | Pentagon denies *Times* story about N-bomb cancellation. |
| West German foreign minister to visit U.S. to urge neutron bomb production. | | Neutron bomb decision is not formally announced. Vance denies a decision was made. Two senators, Nunn and Baker, dissent from Carter's plans. |
| Carter will ask for repeal of embargo against Turkey. | | |
| NATO will increase defense spending 3 percent annually. | | |
| Communist China expresses support for Western European strength. | | |

West Germany was not totally surprised by Carter's decision.

Carter's decision on neutron weapon raises questions among allies over his loyalty.

Carter is rethinking his N-bomb decision. Allies are troubled.

Soviets want N-bomb included in arms limitation talks.

European officials warn Carter not to cancel N-bomb unless Soviets make concessions.

Carter's decision on N-bomb will have bad effect on military establishment.

West German official gives views as to why Carter is reconsidering.

Some Europeans feel Carter gave up N-bomb in order to get arms pact with Soviets.

Brown says N-bomb would help NATO.

Editorial criticizes Carter's decision.

Wednesday, 5

State department and Pentagon officials are pressuring Carter against outright cancellation of neutron weapon. A major factor in Carter's decision was lack of public support for neutron weapon. West Germany's support was too late. Soviets may interpret decision as a sign of weakness.

Thursday, 6

Carter will delay, but not abandon, N-weapon development. N-weapon development is indirectly linked to Soviet behavior. U.S. will also find other new weapons to bolster NATO.

West Germany is most conscious of East bloc threat. Warsaw Pact outnumbers NATO in tanks and men. N-bomb is seen as defensive weapon. Haig underscores this point. But Germany cannot muster enough public support. Uwe Holtz (SPD) indicates his party is against mass-destruction arms.

Vance says Carter will make official announcement of his decision soon. Assorted congressmen take sides on N-bomb issue.

*37*

Friday, 7

Ford and Republicans endorse N-bomb deployment.

Carter announces delay rather than cancellation of N-bomb.

Vance notes that Turkey will permit reopening of U.S. bases if embargo is lifted.

Editorial notes Carter's indecision over N-bomb.

Carter expected to announce decision on N-bomb today. Will also make announcement at NATO council meeting. Pressure from Europeans led to delay rather than canceling of N-bomb. Brown tells Carter that Soviet Backfire deployment makes air defense more important than before.

Republicans discuss N-bomb in banquets in 14 cities. Ford criticizes Carter.

Background report notes that Carter's decision to delay was affected by Europeans. Cost of N-bomb is about $1 million per shell. Soviets are upset about bomb. Carter must think of SALT and MBFR. Some congressmen feel out on a limb because of Carter.

Haig is unhappy. Points out that negotiation cannot work with U.S. making unilateral concessions.

Carter to use A-warhead as bargaining chip with Soviets. NATO allies are unhappy, as is Congress, with Carter's stance.

Carter's delay may offer time to unify NATO on the N-bomb issue. West Germans and Belgians are needed to deploy it. Nunn says Carter's decision will hurt NATO.

Pentagon is upset because N-warhead is useful against Warsaw Pact armor.

NATO is bothered more by the way the decision was made than by decision itself. Carter seems hesitant and uncertain. Schmidt may be in trouble in West Germany, but Dutch seem satisfied.

| | |
|---|---|
| Saturday, 8 | Carter's decision leaves open the chance of reversal of stance. |
| | Britain announces support of Carter's decision. |
| | European leaders still not happy with Carter over decision. |
| | U.S. public more uncertain about Carter now. |
| Sunday, 9 | Senator Byrd notes that a major factor in Carter's decision was European reluctance to deploy weapon. |
| | Carter's decision will cause problems for NATO. |
| | USSR says Carter's decision is insignificant. |
| | Edward Teller explains why N-bomb is necessary. |
| | Drew Middleton discusses controversy over N-warhead. |
| | Carter's decision may embarrass Schmidt. |
| | Editorial is favorable to Carter's decision. |
| | Nitze and Brown take turns attacking and defending Carter. |
| | East Europeans accuse Carter of blackmail, while West Europeans are confused. |
| Monday, 10 | USSR says decision is maneuver to continue N-bomb deployment. |
| | Brown says N-bomb is useful but not necessary. |
| | China says Carter's decision is a result of Soviet propaganda. |
| Tuesday, 11 | Vance says U.S. will sign arms pact with Soviets only if it improves Western security. |
| | Brown says N-bomb is useful but not decisive in defending NATO. |
| Wednesday, 12 | USSR against any trade-off with N-bomb. |

| | |
|---|---|
| Thursday, 13 | Schmidt acknowledges strained relations but welcomes Carter's decision. |
| | Article notes air maneuvers and pilot training for NATO in Alberta. |
| Friday, 14 | Brown assures West Germany that N-bomb decision will not affect military balance. Points out what an acceptable Soviet response would be. |
| | Schmidt explains to West German Parliament his position and why Carter was right. |
| | Op-Ed piece challenges *Times*'s position favorable to N-weapon. |
| Sunday, 16 | Discussion of Dutch Peoples' Party's position against N-bomb. |
| Monday, 17 | British have a manpower shortage that affects their NATO commitment. |
| Tuesday, 18 | Herbert Scoville, former Defense Dept. technical director, speaks against N-bomb. |
| Wednesday, 19 | Denmark bans flights over site of NATO Nuclear Planning Group meeting. |
| | Petition of 1 million Dutch against N-bomb presented to Dutch Parliament. |
| Thursday, 20 | Nuclear Planning Group reacts against Carter's N-bomb decision. |
| | NATO offers USSR concessions on troop reductions. |

40

| | |
|---|---|
| Monday, 24 | Soviets have eased their opposition to sharing of cruise missile technology with NATO allies.<br><br>France denies reports it had exploded an N-bomb. Says no such tests are planned. |
| Tuesday, 25 | Reports of Haig threat to resign due to Carter's N-bomb decision. |
| Wednesday, 26 | Brezhnev outlines Soviet N-bomb position.<br><br>Carter rejects USSR's appeal for joint ban on N-bomb.<br><br>Haig denies resignation threat over N-weapon. Outlines his feelings.<br><br>West Germany wants bigger voice in NATO policies; expresses doubts about U.S. defense policies. |
| Thursday, 27 | U.S. and West German relations are complicated but not bad overall. |
| Friday, 28 | Turkey and communist countries are making more contacts.<br><br>Commander of NATO's southern forces discusses problems and needs of Turkey and Greece in relation to NATO.<br><br>Belgian foreign minister is critical of Carter's decision. |
| Sunday, 30 | Carter discusses lifting of Turkish arms embargo. |

42 / NATO AND THE ATLANTIC DEFENSE

**FIGURE 2.1: New York Times NATO Coverage, 1977 to 1978**

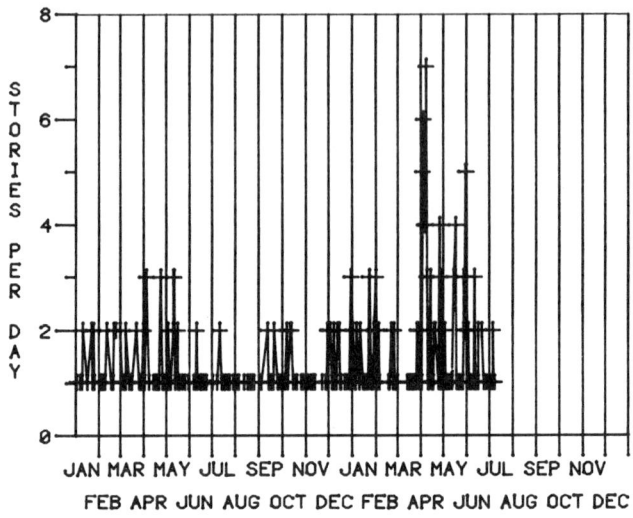

**FIGURE 2.2: CBS News NATO Coverage, 1977 to 1978**

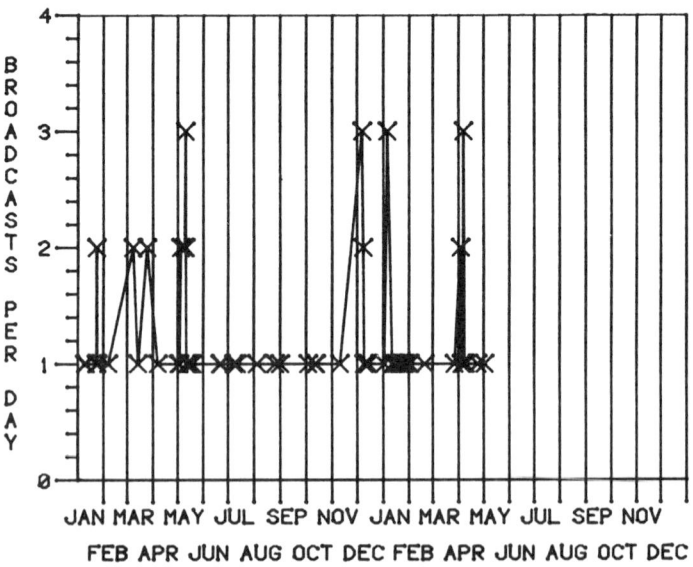

**FIGURE 2.3: Combined CBS News and New York Times NATO Coverage, April 1978**

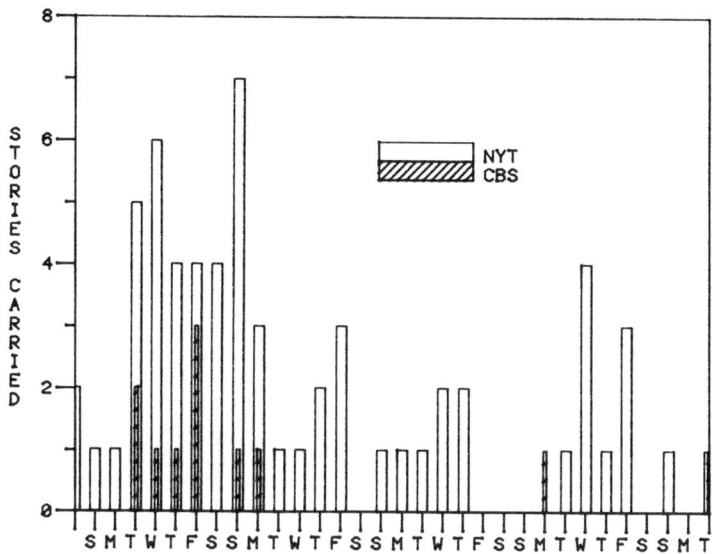

is the distinct impression that the Germans, especially, wanted the United States to give the appearance of forcing the neutron weapon on Europe, rather like a maiden who wanted to be forcefully taken, but taken nonetheless.

The imagery of the above simile is not entirely facetious since it fits into a long-term U.S. image of Europe. NATO and Europe, in both media, are used interchangeably, and the word "entangling" to describe the nature of the alliance would certainly occur to any reader or viewer of these two media. Both European nations and their politicians come over as being somewhat more clever than the Americans and their leader. Yet the wily Europeans do not emerge in either medium as unprincipled. Instead, the opponents of the neutron weapon, German and Dutch for the most part, come over as peace-loving types trying to avoid a nuclear holocaust.

## CONCLUSIONS

What conclusions can be drawn from the examination and analysis of the NATO image projected in the United States, including possible effects on American public opinion?

First, the public image is generally favorable, but this support given to NATO is not devoid of criticism. What is expected from other NATO allies are appropriate financial contributions to the common defense effort, some kind of improved system of weapons standardization and procurement, and a generally cooperative attitude of all NATO member governments. This applies to the Greek-Turkish dispute, where the U.S. Congress played an unfortunate role, as well as to the reluctance of Belgium and the Netherlands to accept the nuclear theater weapons very recently. Cross-Atlantic production of weapons, such as the manufacture of the F-16 fighter plane, is perceived as a proper example of improved weapons procurement and production as are similar intra-European efforts. However, there are in all NATO countries linkages between domestic and foreign policies that militate at times against rational procurement and standardization decisions, and the resulting pressure politics are well understood in the United States. On the other hand, the perception that U.S. taxpayers still must generally shoulder a heavier burden than their counterparts in other NATO countries tends to impair somewhat the image of transatlantic harmony (as will be seen in Chapters 4 and 6), but this does not detract from the recognition that a strong NATO is desirable and indeed necessary.

Second, NATO's security function is always portrayed foremost by the U.S. news media. This should not be surprising since the media, especially television, must focus on "action" coverage to attract readers and viewers, and therefore show prime interest in every type of crisis. Readership indifference is a disincentive to publishing a greater diversity of NATO items. Therefore other functions of NATO that the Information Service is interested in extolling, such as political consultation and seeking solutions for the challenges of modern society, have difficulty finding their way into the news media.

Finally, this analysis shows the impact of geography on news coverage. The greater the distance from the Atlantic area, the lower the coverage. This most likely means that peoples' perceptions of what is important are affected by geographical distances and that newspaper editions, sensitive to this phenomenon, must make decisions about the newsworthiness of an event at every phase of the media production process. Hence, to compensate for greater distance, occurrences in nonproximate countries will have to meet more stringent criteria before being considered newsworthy. They must be perceived as particularly threatening by the prospective audience or especially desirable, or, as a minimum, particularly spectacular.

# 3

# THE IMPACT OF NATO-PRODUCED FILMS

While the image of NATO in the United States can be influenced only indirectly, and perhaps only marginally, by press conferences and communiques emanating from the NATO Information Services in Brussels and by various news stories appearing in newspapers and periodicals and shown on television, another medium offers a potentially greater effect: films produced by NATO Information Services.

Broadcasts of NATO-produced films, such as *Borealis, Europe-America,* or *The Great Highway*, could be potentially very effective in enhancing the image of NATO. In contrast to news items, the films constitute deliberate efforts of influencing audiences to accept and adopt values considered as supporting and strengthening the pursuit of NATO goals. Their impact depends less upon immediacy than on dramatic production techniques; they are an art form as well as political-military documentaries.

In the United States, it is difficult to circulate these kinds of films for purposes of television broadcasting. On commercial stations, it is difficult to find nationwide or even regional sponsors for NATO films. On educational stations, the prevailing ideology seems to be antithetical to footage smacking of "militarism." All in all, it is not common to see these films broadcast on network or public stations serving areas large enough to be designated as a standard metropolitan statistical area (SMSA) by the Bureau of Census.

On the other hand, NATO films do receive attention from small network affiliates and cablecasters, as well as an occasional broadcast on the educational television station in the South. The data available are displayed to best advantage cartographically rather than statistically because this method provides a much clearer illustration of the areas reached with NATO films. Figures 3.1 through 3.5 are suggestive of the work being done with such displays. These maps are "thematic" in nature, that is, they suggest a pattern rather than conform to a rigid mathematical model. Nonetheless, this presentation can be rendered more precise and may offer a suitable method of evaluating the impact of various films.

In this series of maps, the vertical dimension is proportional to the number of viewers, as is the case of the map of newspaper articles (Figure 3.1) that is included here for comparison purposes. There are a number of striking features to this map series. These maps are based on the tables in Appendix A that summarize data provided by NATO's film agent in the United States. From those tables alone, however, it is difficult to determine any geographical pattern or, indeed, any statistical pattern. In this sense, the maps make it possible to fully appreciate the meaning of these data.

A second feature to note is that the films do not conform to the East-West pattern of newspaper coverage. Instead, the films do rather well in the Pacific West and in the Confederate Southeast (Tennessee, Mississippi, and Alabama). Basically, the films are not redundant to newspaper coverage but open up a new market so to speak.

Another striking aspect was the lack of attention to NATO films by the Public Broadcasting System (PBS). PBS has greatly improved in the United States in the last few years (mainly, some argue, through purchases of BBC series such as "Masterpiece Theatre"). Still, NATO films are documentary in nature, and one is hard pressed to find an easy explanation for the fact that the only PBS station showing a NATO film was found in Baton Rogue, Louisiana. One might venture the hypothesis that PBS is suffering from memories of battles with the Nixon administration and so has an understandable anti-institutional basis. No doubt, PBS officials would deny this and so would local station management. But PBS viewers are no strangers to Soviet productions that occasionally have a heavy-handed political message.

A final point that bears mentioning is the frequency with which NATO films are carried by Cable Television (CATV) or cablecasters. CATV is growing with remarkable speed in the United States. Originally, it amounted to nothing more than a hard-wired rural television service for ranchers and farmers. Later on, it was found that cable was useful in the most urbanized areas where home antennas are often not suitable due to the interference caused by skyscrapers. Since cable has become more popular, it has grown from a simple rebroadcast of local programs by means of a superior antenna to a system of its own involving programming from distant stations, first-run movies, sports, news, and even religion through closed-circuit channels. Understandably, cable companies have an adversary relationship with the networks. Both may have an adversary relationship with datavision, an even newer form of television

**FIGURE 3.1: Newspaper Coverage, 1977 to 1978**

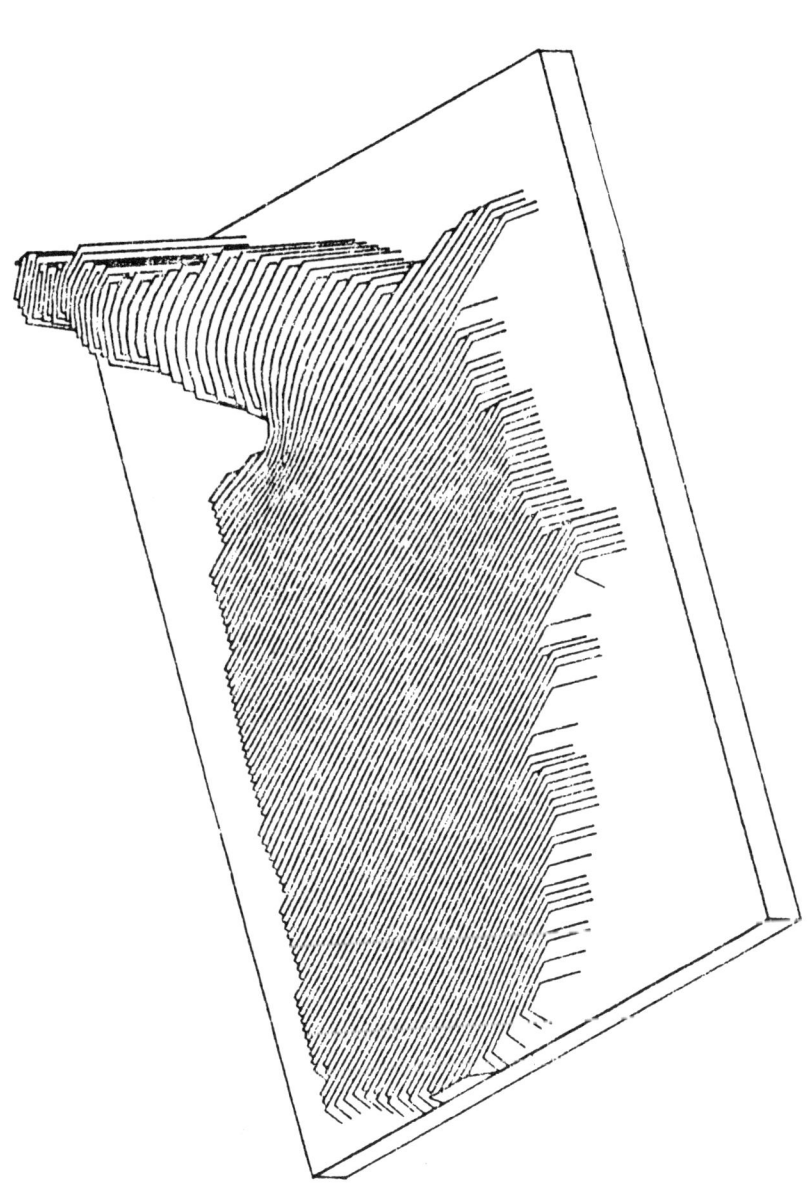

## FIGURE 3.2: 1978 Showings of The Great Highway

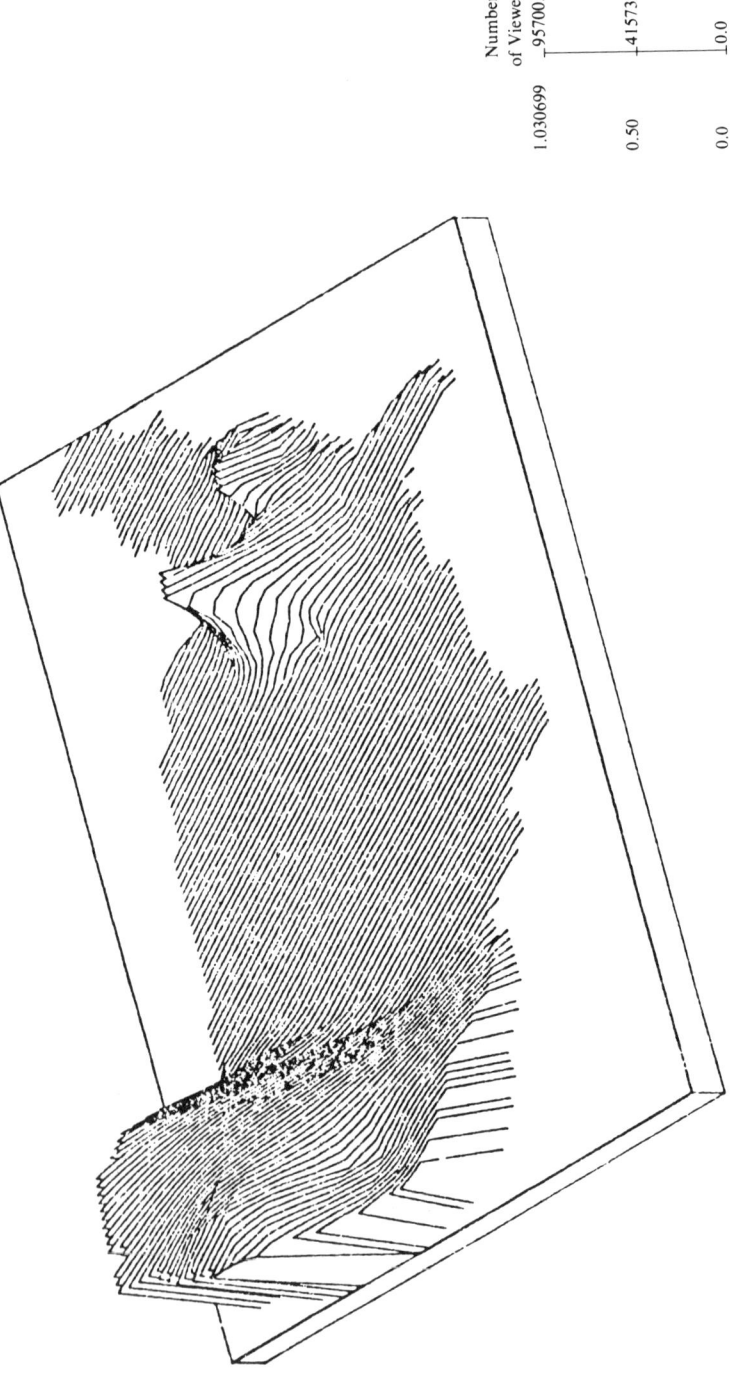

**FIGURE 3.3: 1978 Showings of <u>Borealis</u>**

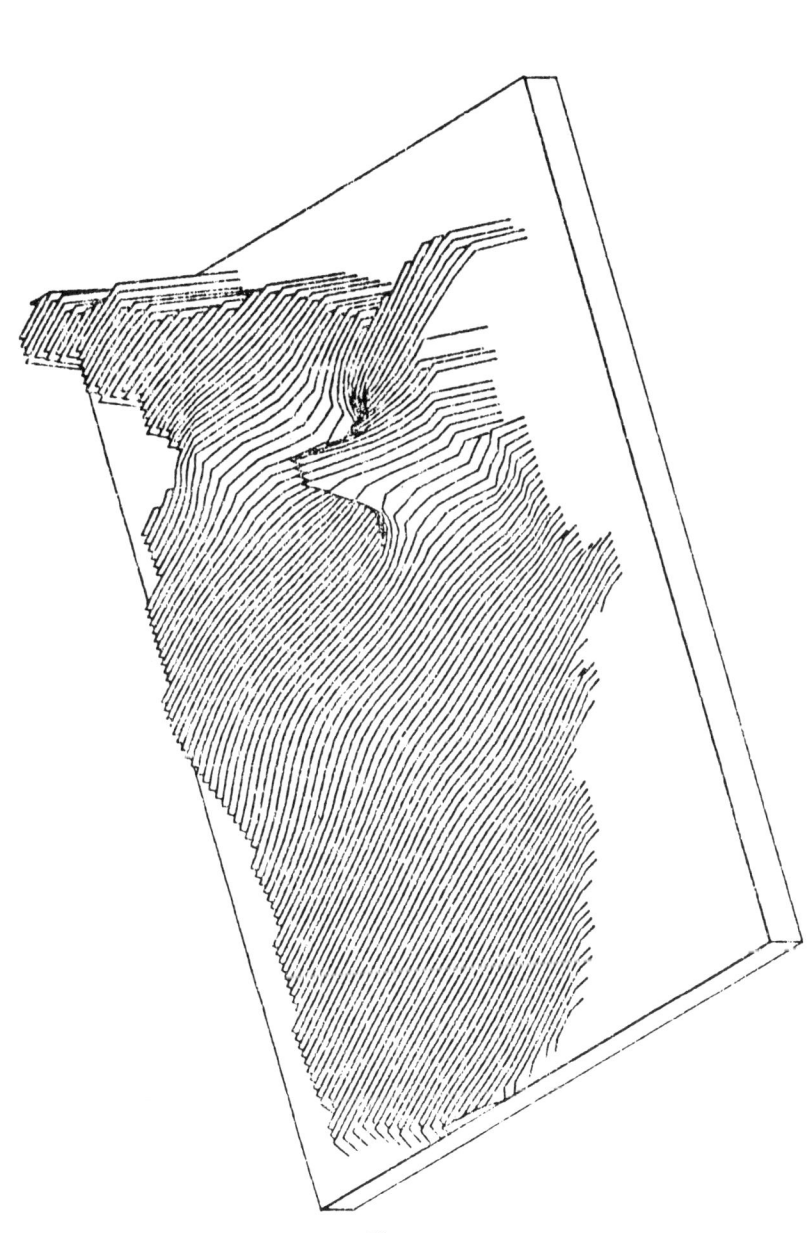

**FIGURE 3.4: 1978 Showings of Europe and America**

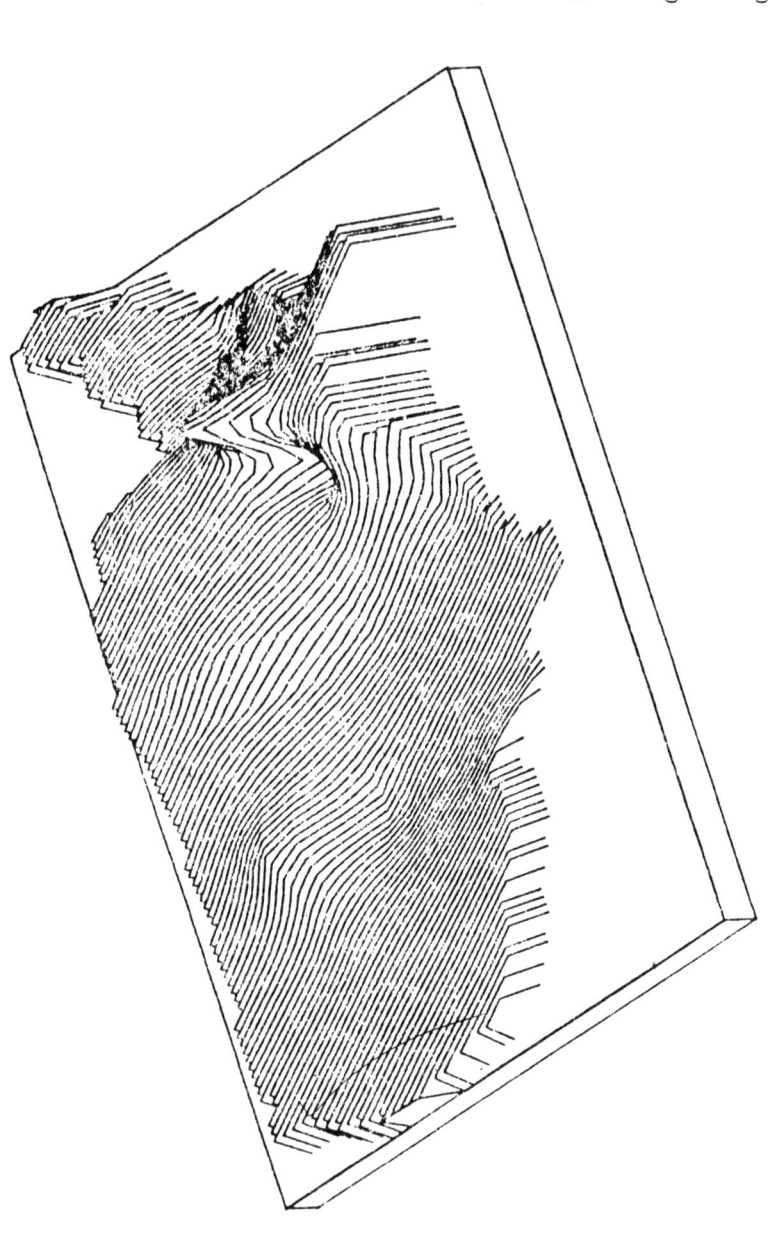

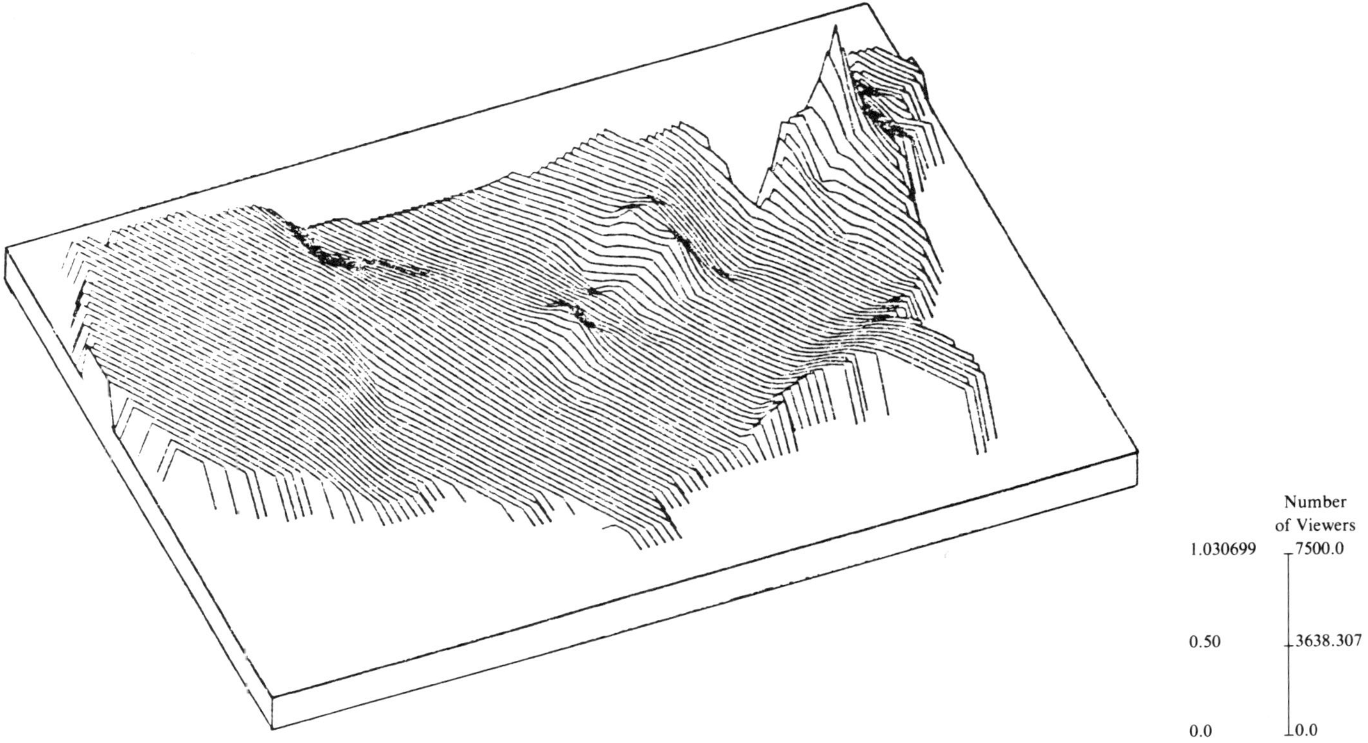

FIGURE 3.5: 1978 Showings of New Version of Europe and America

that exists in Europe but has not yet been licensed in the United States. In any event, the cable companies are hungry for footage and for a public service image. NATO films seem to fit these needs. Moreover, the films seem to find sympathetic audiences in rural American towns served by cable. This changing technology provides an opportunity to NATO and a challenge to produce truly marketable films.

## A TEST OF A NATO FILM

The demand for NATO films by television stations provides a measurement of interest on the part of viewers in NATO activities and may even reflect a measure of support. However, it does not offer a basis on which to evaluate the film's effectiveness in attaining the objectives of the producers, except in a very broad sense. In order to make such an evaluation, a controlled experiment was conducted in September 1979 with respect to NATO's latest film, *Lives*. This film depicts NATO as a major tool for safeguarding the democratic way of life and Western values by focusing on selected families in a number of NATO countries, including the United States, and showing how various aspects of NATO affect their lives.

This experiment, which can be replicated in other places, tested the effects of the film on the judgment, affect, and cognition of nearly 400 students (mostly first- and second-year students) who viewed the film and completed a structured questionnaire. A copy of this questionnaire can be found in Appendix B. In particular, the authors wanted to learn whether the film made a difference in:

How viewers *evaluate* their nation's commitment to defense, particularly with respect to NATO, relative to other national priorities;

How viewers *like* the NATO allies—the people living in other NATO countries; and

How much viewers *know* about NATO.

A questionnaire was constructed that covered all three aspects of the film's potential impact. The first 29 questions pertained to the evaluative aspect and included: general questions about political perceptions and national spending priorities; philosophical questions regarding war; and specific questions on NATO. This was followed by a test of the students' feelings toward the nationals of various countries, both NATO members and others.* Finally,

---

*The countries were the Soviet Union, Japan, England, Canada, Brazil, the Peoples' Republic of China, Israel, Egypt, France, Italy, Poland, West Germany, Holland, East Germany, Mexico, Saudi Arabia, Belgium, Iran, Sweden, Spain, Portugal, Norway, Switzerland, and Denmark (see also Appendix B).

an attempt was made to assess the film's cognition effect by inquiring into the students' knowledge as to which countries are members of NATO. Since the film does not deal with issues of organization, strategy, or logistics, it was not useful to cover other cognition objects.

The students were divided into two groups, numbering initially 200 and 114 individuals. The number of students in the groups varied between the first and third day of the test, which is a normal occurrence in all university classes. The first group was designated the control group; its members filled out the questionnaire prior to seeing the film. Three days later, they were shown the film and immediately afterward were asked to fill out the questionnaire again. The second administration of the questionnaire was labeled "retest." The second group of students was called the experimental group; its members saw the film one day, but were not asked to fill out the questionnaire until three days later. It took between 15 and 23 minutes to answer the questionnaire.

**Test Results**

The results of the test clearly indicate that the film had a positive impact on the students, but the effects were not evenly distributed over all aspects tested. The details of the results may be gleaned from five tables: the replies to the general priorities questions (1-17) are found in Table 3.1; the philosophical questions on war (21-27) in Table 3.2; the specific questions pertaining to NATO (18-20, 28, 29) in Table 3.3; and the answers to the affect and cognition questions are found in Tables 3.4 and 3.5 respectively.

*Evaluation Segment*

Table 3.1 shows not only the responses of the students on the national priorities questions, but also the results from the nationwide survey conducted in 1978 by the National Opinion Research Center of the University of Chicago. The student respondents have a generally more favorable view of the political and governmental system than suggested by the nationwide survey. They feel that more governmental resources should be devoted to the defense effort than does the public at large, but express sentiments similar to the national sample with respect to the environment, urban affairs, and the rising crime rate. On the other hand, they complain that too many resources are allocated to public welfare. This suggests a group of respondents that is rather conservative, but the replies also reflect their urban and overwhelmingly lower-middle-class backgrounds. The changes in the replies of the experimental and retest groups relative to those of the control group are minimal and insignificant which, of course, is not surprising. Nevertheless, the answers to this cluster of questions are important because they establish the nature of the students who were tested.

**TABLE 3.1: Responses to Political Evaluation and National Spending Priority Questions (percent)**

Perceptions about Politics

1. "People like me don't have any say about what government does."

|  | Control Group | Experimental Group | Retest Group | National Opinion |
|---|---|---|---|---|
| Agree | 25 | 27 | 19 | 42 |
| Disagree | 75 | 73 | 81 | 58 |
| N | 246 | 125 | 227 | NA |

2. "Voting is the only way that people like me can have any say."

|  | Control Group | Experimental Group | Retest Group | National Opinion |
|---|---|---|---|---|
| Agree | 38 | 27 | 32 | 56 |
| Disagree | 62 | 73 | 68 | 44 |
| N | 245 | 127 | 224 | NA |

3. "Sometimes politics and government seem so complicated."

|  | Control Group | Experimental Group | Retest Group | National Opinion |
|---|---|---|---|---|
| Agree | 70 | 66 | 65 | 73 |
| Disagree | 30 | 34 | 35 | 27 |
| N | 246 | 126 | 225 | NA |

4. "I don't think public officials care much what people like me think."

|  | Control Group | Experimental Group | Retest Group | National Opinion |
|---|---|---|---|---|
| Agree | 54 | 46 | 44 | 54 |
| Disagree | 46 | 54 | 56 | 46 |
| N | 241 | 123 | 222 | NA |

5. "Those we elect to Congress in Washington lose touch with people."

|  | Control Group | Experimental Group | Retest Group | National Opinion |
|---|---|---|---|---|
| Agree | 73 | 73 | 65 | 72 |
| Disagree | 27 | 27 | 35 | 28 |
| N | 239 | 121 | 220 | NA |

6. "Parties are only interested in people's votes, not in their opinions."

|  | Control Group | Experimental Group | Retest Group | National Opinion |
|---|---|---|---|---|
| Agree | 59 | 61 | 53 | 64 |
| Disagree | 41 | 39 | 47 | 46 |
| N | 244 | 126 | 224 | NA |

## Spending Priorities

7. Research and science

|  | Control Group | Experimental Group | Retest Group | National Opinion |
|---|---|---|---|---|
| Too little | 41 | 46 | 37 | 14 |
| About right | 47 | 41 | 55 | 37 |
| Too much | 12 | 13 | 8 | 49 |
| N | 191 | 102 | 211 | 1,436 |

8. Improving environment

|  | Control Group | Experimental Group | Retest Group | National Opinion |
|---|---|---|---|---|
| Too little | 68 | 75 | 70 | 55 |
| About right | 27 | 23 | 26 | 34 |
| Too much | 5 | 2 | 4 | 11 |
| N | 227 | 113 | 218 | 1,448 |

9. Improving health

|  | Control Group | Experimental Group | Retest Group | National Opinion |
|---|---|---|---|---|
| Too little | 59 | 59 | 55 | 58 |
| About right | 37 | 34 | 41 | 35 |
| Too much | 4 | 7 | 4 | 7 |
| N | 227 | 111 | 212 | 1,471 |

10. Solving problems of big cities

|  | Control Group | Experimental Group | Retest Group | National Opinion |
|---|---|---|---|---|
| Too little | 67 | 60 | 61 | 44 |
| About right | 23 | 33 | 29 | 34 |
| Too much | 10 | 7 | 10 | 22 |
| N | 202 | 102 | 196 | 1,334 |

11. Halting crime rate

|  | Control Group | Experimental Group | Retest Group | National Opinion |
|---|---|---|---|---|
| Too little | 87 | 85 | 82 | 68 |
| About right | 12 | 12 | 16 | 26 |
| Too much | 1 | 3 | 2 | 6 |
| N | 227 | 116 | 215 | 1,460 |

12. Dealing with drug addiction

|  | Control Group | Experimental Group | Retest Group | National Opinion |
|---|---|---|---|---|
| Too little | 49 | 40 | 46 | 58 |
| About right | 41 | 41 | 45 | 33 |
| Too much | 10 | 19 | 9 | 9 |
| N | 213 | 104 | 205 | 1,452 |

13. Improving education

|  | Control Group | Experimental Group | Retest Group | National Opinion |
|---|---|---|---|---|
| Too little | 75 | 83 | 75 | 54 |
| About right | 22 | 14 | 24 | 35 |
| Too much | 3 | 3 | 1 | 11 |
| N | 238 | 127 | 221 | 1,472 |

14. Improving blacks' condition

|  | Control Group | Experimental Group | Retest Group | National Opinion |
|---|---|---|---|---|
| Too little | 32 | 34 | 30 | 26 |
| About right | 22 | 19 | 31 | 47 |
| Too much | 46 | 47 | 39 | 27 |
| N | 223 | 111 | 204 | 1,417 |

15. Arms and defense

|  | Control Group | Experimental Group | Retest Group | National Opinion |
|---|---|---|---|---|
| Too little | 34 | 35 | 31 | 29 |
| About right | 39 | 35 | 48 | 47 |
| Too much | 27 | 30 | 21 | 24 |
| N | 226 | 119 | 208 | 1,473 |

16. Foreign aid

|  | Control Group | Experimental Group | Retest Group | National Opinion |
|---|---|---|---|---|
| Too little | 6 | 3 | 5 | 4 |
| About right | 17 | 16 | 29 | 25 |
| Too much | 77 | 81 | 66 | 71 |
| N | 225 | 115 | 211 | 1,444 |

17. Welfare

|  | Control Group | Experimental Group | Retest Group | National Opinion |
|---|---|---|---|---|
| Too little | 15 | 14 | 14 | 14 |
| About right | 24 | 12 | 27 | 26 |
| Too much | 61 | 74 | 59 | 60 |
| N | 229 | 119 | 208 | 1,473 |

With respect to the philosophical views on war (Table 3.2), there was a minor positive effect of the film on the retest group, especially in the questions on the possibility of war and the practicability of pacifism. Otherwise, the effects seem to be somewhat ambiguous.

A very positive impact of the film, however, is evident in the replies to the NATO-related questions by both the experimental and retest groups (Table 3.3). Thus one can generalize that none of the groups tested showed either a predominantly hawkish or dovish attitude. By and large, the students have a fairly moderate sort of Teddy Roosevelt "speak softly but carry a big stick" attitude. Importantly, defending NATO allies is very popular; there is no desire to let Europe fend for itself, and there is substantial feeling that the United States would be weaker without the alliance with Western Europe. These attitudes have been significantly strengthened by the film.

*Affect*

In the area of affect, students were asked to rate countries from −5 to +5 in terms of whether they liked or disliked them very much. These countries included allies, actual or potential adversaries, and nonaligned nations throughout the world. These data on affect were analyzed with a battery of statistical tools. But even larger samples would have, at best, given more assurances that only minor differences exist. Indeed, the impact of the film on the responses of the students appears to be very minor and somewhat ambiguous as well.

In specific cases, the results are curious. With respect to the Soviet Union, the experimental group was significantly less hostile than the control

## TABLE 3.2: Responses to Philosophical Questions on War (percent)

| | Control Group | Experimental Group | Retest Group |
|---|---|---|---|
| **21. Run any risk of war to stop communism** | | | |
| Agree strongly | 27 | 22 | 24 |
| Agree somewhat | 39 | 35 | 45 |
| Disagree somewhat | 24 | 21 | 21 |
| Disagree strongly | 10 | 22 | 10 |
| N | 232 | 122 | 217 |
| **22. Begin unilateral gradual disarmament** | | | |
| Agree strongly | 2 | 3 | 4 |
| Agree somewhat | 13 | 15 | 17 |
| Disagree somewhat | 23 | 18 | 24 |
| Disagree strongly | 62 | 64 | 55 |
| N | 214 | 109 | 207 |
| **23. Pacifist demonstrations hurt our best interests** | | | |
| Agree strongly | 12 | 9 | 9 |
| Agree somewhat | 29 | 34 | 34 |
| Disagree somewhat | 29 | 30 | 34 |
| Disagree strongly | 30 | 27 | 23 |
| N | 221 | 115 | 209 |
| **24. No moral principles exist to risk destruction of mankind in struggle with communism** | | | |
| Agree strongly | 27 | 21 | 20 |
| Agree somewhat | 26 | 28 | 26 |
| Disagree somewhat | 21 | 27 | 33 |
| Disagree strongly | 26 | 24 | 21 |
| N | 215 | 117 | 200 |
| **25. To participate in war and kill others is immoral** | | | |
| Agree strongly | 28 | 24 | 29 |
| Agree somewhat | 20 | 24 | 25 |
| Disagree somewhat | 25 | 26 | 27 |
| Disagree strongly | 27 | 26 | 19 |
| N | 220 | 115 | 209 |
| **26. Real enemy is no longer communism but war itself** | | | |
| Agree strongly | 39 | 39 | 33 |
| Agree somewhat | 35 | 32 | 42 |
| Disagree somewhat | 14 | 16 | 15 |
| Disagree strongly | 12 | 13 | 8 |
| N | 234 | 118 | 213 |
| **27. Pacifism is not practical** | | | |
| Agree strongly | 22 | 24 | 20 |
| Agree somewhat | 35 | 35 | 44 |
| Disagree somewhat | 32 | 28 | 26 |
| Disagree strongly | 11 | 13 | 10 |
| N | 172 | 95 | 160 |

## TABLE 3.3: Responses to NATO-Related Questions (percent)

| | Control Group | Experimental Group | Retest Group |
|---|---|---|---|
| 18. About the chances of U.S. getting into war | | | |
| Pretty worried | 22 | 19 | 18 |
| Somewhat worried | 59 | 59 | 63 |
| Not worried | 19 | 26 | 19 |
| N | 240 | 126 | 227 |
| 19. U.S. troops in Europe | | | |
| Bring home most of them | 15 | 14 | 10 |
| Keep about the same number there | 70 | 75 | 79 |
| Send more troops | 15 | 11 | 11 |
| N | 235 | 124 | 225 |
| 20. SALT Treaty ratification | | | |
| OK the treaty as it is | 13 | 15 | 16 |
| OK with reservations & amendments | 70 | 71 | 71 |
| Reject the treaty entirely | 17 | 14 | 13 |
| N | 218 | 119 | 217 |
| 28. On defending the U.S. and alliance with NATO | | | |
| U.S. would be weaker without NATO | 80 | 83 | 92 |
| Blocs like NATO threaten peace | 20 | 18 | 8 |
| N | 226 | 83 | 213 |
| 29. On the defense of Europe and on NATO | | | |
| Europeans should fend for themselves | 21 | 13 | 8 |
| NATO helps protect our way of life | 79 | 87 | 92 |
| N | 225 | 86 | 218 |

group, but the retest group in turn showed a much more hostile attitude than either other group. Similar trends can be noticed on the responses to China, Poland, and East Germany, as well as to Japan and Saudi Arabia. Another curious result pertains to Denmark, where the responses of both the experimental and retest groups are more negative, while on Norway the retest group reversed slightly the very negative trend of the experimental group. The opposite is shown with respect to Belgium. On the other hand, the trend of the responses regarding Canada, Italy, and the Federal Republic of Germany become more positive in both groups after seeing the film, which is more in accordance with the film producers' expectation.

*Cognition*

The impact of *Lives* on the student respondents' knowledge of NATO membership is unmistakable. The control group correctly identified an average of three allies, the experimental group 4.3 allies, and the retest group 4.5 allies. Put in the odd language of statistics, it seems that viewing *Lives* makes a student aware of another ally-and-a-half. Actually, things are even better than that, since this scoring system takes into account nonallies (such as Sweden or Mexico) that students often mistake for allies (for details, see Table 3.4).

One cannot but bemoan the ignorance students have of allied nations. Of course, if they knew more about their allies, *Lives* would be a superfluous effort. Still, aside from the cognitive impact of *Lives*, what implications does it or any other knowledge-imparting device have apropos to NATO? The experiment did not suggest that after viewing *Lives* students became xenophobic toward Soviet bloc nations—nor xenophilous toward NATO allies. There was no sign that the control group was "dovish," nor any suggestion that the experimental group became "hawkish." There seems to be no direct relationship between *Lives* and defense-related attitudes.

The familiarity of students with allies is positively correlated with feelings about increased defense spending. Of those students least familiar with allies (zero to two correct responses), 26 percent felt the United States was spending too little on arms; of those who could identify three or more allies, 35 percent felt it was spending too little. This general feeling about arms expenditures is directly related to the U.S. presence in Europe. The data revealed overwhelming support among all groups of students for the current level of troop commitment, but the least familiar group had only 8 percent willingness to advocate increasing U.S. units in Europe, while the more informed group had

**TABLE 3.4: Cognition of Allies (percent)**

| Perceived as an Ally | Control Group | Experimental Group | Retest Group |
|---|---|---|---|
| Canada | 83 | 90 | 90 |
| Mexico | 49 | 46 | 50 |
| Luxembourg | 51 | 51 | 69 |
| Iceland | 54 | 80 | 71 |
| Switzerland | 57 | 46 | 46 |
| Portugal | 42 | 59 | 74 |
| Turkey | 41 | 69 | 67 |
| Greece | 50 | 69 | 67 |
| Sweden | 65 | 53 | 56 |
| Denmark | 71 | 64 | 76 |
| England | 88 | 92 | 93 |
| Italy | 71 | 82 | 79 |
| Spain | 63 | 57 | 72 |
| West Germany | 69 | 74 | 77 |

more than 14 percent support for this action. In a similar vein, more than 19 percent of the least informed students thought that Europe should fend for itself in a crisis, an idea that only 12 percent of the more informed shared (see Table 3.5).

These differences are not dramatic; they hardly suggest that *Lives* polarizes its viewers. Even though the film does show an ability to inform and familiarize students with allies and leads to a more sympathetic view of collective defense, there is no sign that it affects students' basic attitudes toward war and peace. A set of questions were asked about pacifist activities, including the risk of world destruction and disarmament, to name a few. These questions tap a basic moral dimension. On these questions, levels of cognition showed no correlation with attitudes: most students reject unilateral disarmament, do not think pacifist activities are harmful, and are split about evenly on how far the United States should go in risking world destruction. By and large, *Lives* does not create warmongering advocates of a garrison state that suppresses dissent.

## SUMMARY AND CONCLUSIONS

The findings suggest that the film *Lives* does have a favorable impact on the judgment of the students tested with respect to NATO-related issues of defense. In this respect, the film attains one of its major objectives. On the other hand, it had only a very minor influence on the students' philosophical attitudes regarding war, but some bearing on the choices of national priorities. Most likely, nothing else could be anticipated from the nature of the film. As has been see, a favorable prodefense bias is already clearly visible in the responses of the students.

In the affective area, the film does not create any stronger pro-West European sentiments—indeed, they are already pretty strong. It also does not bolster to any significant degree the existing Russophobia that is fairly substantial.

In terms of cognition, a convincing case has been made that a film like *Lives* is useful for getting across information about who is in NATO, although this is hardly the theme of the film. Still, films can, as a beneficial by-product, inform the audience even when that is not their goal.

From a statistical point of view, a film such as *Lives* does not provide a rapid-fire stimulus. Its effects are more subtle and somewhat downstream in terms of time. Years from now it may make a difference for Americans to have seen the film and have in their memories the notion that Europeans are "real people."

Lastly, the authors believe that the instrument they used is basically adequate; it is well founded in theory and has good wording. Moreover, it is

## TABLE 3.5: Cognition and Defense: NATO-Related Issues (percent)

|  | Students' correct identification of allies | | |
|---|---|---|---|
|  | 0-2 | 3-4 | 4 or more |
| 15. Arms and defense | | | |
| Too little | 26 | 39 | 35 |
| About right | 50 | 38 | 38 |
| Too much | 24 | 23 | 27 |
| N | 165 | 152 | 246 |
| 18. About the chances of U.S. getting into war | | | |
| Pretty worried | 16 | 20 | 22 |
| Somewhat worried | 60 | 61 | 58 |
| Not worried | 24 | 19 | 20 |
| N | 178 | 161 | 254 |
| 19. U.S. troops in Europe | | | |
| Bring home | 16 | 10 | 12 |
| Keep same | 76 | 75 | 74 |
| Increment | 8 | 15 | 14 |
| N | 170 | 162 | 252 |
| 20. SALT Treaty ratification | | | |
| OK as is | 15 | 11 | 17 |
| Amend | 72 | 73 | 69 |
| Reject | 13 | 16 | 14 |
| N | 160 | 149 | 245 |
| 21. Run any risk of war | | | |
| Agree strongly | 27 | 25 | 24 |
| Agree somewhat | 46 | 39 | 37 |
| Disagree somewhat | 16 | 25 | 24 |
| Disagree strongly | 11 | 11 | 15 |
| N | 166 | 157 | 248 |
| 22. Begin unilateral gradual disarmament | | | |
| Agree strongly | 5 | 1 | 3 |
| Agree somewhat | 13 | 18 | 15 |
| Disagree somewhat | 28 | 22 | 19 |
| Disagree strongly | 54 | 59 | 63 |
| N | 151 | 143 | 236 |
| 23. Pacifist demonstrations hurt our best interests | | | |
| Agree strongly | 9 | 13 | 9 |
| Agree somewhat | 33 | 27 | 34 |
| Disagree somewhat | 29 | 36 | 30 |
| Disagree strongly | 29 | 24 | 27 |
| N | 160 | 149 | 236 |

24. No moral principles exist to risk destruction of mankind in struggle with communism

|  |  |  |  |
|---|---|---|---|
| Agree strongly | 25 | 20 | 23 |
| Agree somewhat | 24 | 28 | 27 |
| Disagree somewhat | 28 | 22 | 30 |
| Disagree strongly | 23 | 30 | 20 |
| N | 149 | 148 | 235 |

25. To participate in war and kill others is immoral

|  |  |  |  |
|---|---|---|---|
| Agree strongly | 25 | 32 | 26 |
| Agree somewhat | 25 | 21 | 23 |
| Disagree somewhat | 29 | 20 | 27 |
| Disagree strongly | 21 | 27 | 24 |
| N | 159 | 149 | 236 |

26. Real enemy is no longer communism but war itself

|  |  |  |  |
|---|---|---|---|
| Agree strongly | 41 | 37 | 36 |
| Agree somewhat | 37 | 36 | 38 |
| Disagree somewhat | 15 | 17 | 13 |
| Disagree strongly | 7 | 10 | 13 |
| N | 167 | 154 | 244 |

27. Pacifism is not practical

|  |  |  |  |
|---|---|---|---|
| Agree strongly | 17 | 23 | 23 |
| Agree somewhat | 48 | 36 | 34 |
| Disagree somewhat | 25 | 34 | 29 |
| Disagree strongly | 10 | 7 | 14 |
| N | 113 | 116 | 198 |

28. On defending the U.S. and alliance with NATO

|  |  |  |  |
|---|---|---|---|
| U.S. would be weaker without NATO | 84 | 86 | 86 |
| Blocs like NATO threaten peace | 16 | 14 | 14 |
| N | 153 | 146 | 223 |

29. On the defense of Europe and on NATO

|  |  |  |  |
|---|---|---|---|
| Europeans should fend for themselves | 19 | 13 | 12 |
| NATO helps protect our way of life | 81 | 87 | 88 |
| N | 156 | 149 | 224 |

short, quick to code, and easy to interpret in terms of results. That being the case, other films that may be somewhat more dramatic (involving tanks, fighters, amphibious landings, and a few menacing Red Army platoons) might show different effects from this rather subtle but very well-done *Lives*.

In more general terms, it seems that NATO films are basically useful means to inform the American public (mass and elite) about NATO's functions, such as safeguarding democratic values in the polities of the member states. However, the geographic distribution pattern of these films suggests that even for this medium the audiences are limited, and prime viewing time is often not available. Nevertheless, if audiences can be found for the films, and perhaps expanded in numbers, a definite favorable impact can be produced as this test of *Lives* has demonstrated.

# 4

# PUBLIC OPINION ABOUT DEFENSE AND NATO AND MEDIA INFLUENCE

So far this volume has analyzed the intensity and extent of media coverage of NATO and reported on the impact of selected NATO films distributed in the United States. It has been seen that as a result of printed and video news, the image of NATO projected in the United States is complex but generally sympathetic. This chapter will look at the attitudes and media output reactions of the general public and elites regarding defense, security, and, as far as possible, NATO.

This chapter will explore four major sources of data:

- National Opinion Research Center (NORC) data, primarily its General Social Survey (GSS);
- Chicago Council on Foreign Relations (CCFR), survey of foreign policy attitudes 1974 and 1978;
- Gallup poll survey conducted for the Atlantic Council of the United States in fall 1980; and
- Foreign Policy Association (FPA) of the United States' "Great Decisions" program.

By and large, U.S. polls do not concentrate on foreign affairs, but some very high quality data are available. One major source is a continuing series of what are called "omnibus" polls taken by the National Opinion Research Center. Data from its General Social Survey extend from 1972 through 1980 in the currently available format. The great advantage of these annual polls is that they repeat many questions each year so one can see the direction opinion is taking, as well as where it is located. The second source, the Chicago Council on Foreign Relations, has hired the Gallup Organization to do the polling. Utilizing the data on tape for 1974 and the CCFR official summary for the 1978 data (published in 1979), the authors were able to make comparisons between the two years, although the technical quality of the comparisons is somewhat constrained. The 1980 Gallup questions are concerned with attitudes toward NATO and the extent of American willingness to engage in combat. In the Foreign Policy Association's "Great Decisions" program, interested members of the public read FPA-prepared essays on selected topics and meet for seminar-type discussions. Subsequently, they fill out ballot forms in which various alternate responses to problems are presented.

## U.S. FOREIGN POLICY ATTITUDES AND CONSTITUENCIES

One of the most common observations made about Americans by visiting Europeans, or by Europeans who encounter traveling Americans, is that Americans betray a wide ignorance of foreign affairs that often seems based on a conscious and perverse disinclination to expand their horizons. Americans emerge as uninformed, naive, and unsophisticated when it comes to international politics. Furthermore, they speak nothing but English, and hardly the English that Europeans learned in their schools or in summers in Britain.

There is a good deal of accuracy in this impression—at least in terms of matters of fact. Americans do not know much about what happens in Europe. They are unfamiliar with political figures and processes. They have little sense of Europe's geographical scale. They have very little sense of what it means to be bordered by the Soviet Union. They would be horrified at the thought of a strong domestic Communist Party. Finally, Europe's babble of languages seems like a needless complication that makes it harder to do business.

But observant Europeans soon understand that Americans have a sophistication of their own that is well adapted to the New World. Americans have forged a multiethnic but fundamentally monolingual nation that spans a continent. The government is no more effective on a day-to-day basis than many European governments, but it is hard to find anywhere governments that enjoy the unquestioned legitimacy found in the United States. A democratic government spanning an entire continent that has stood the test of more than two centuries is an achievement that continues to evoke admiration in many parts of the free world.

The endurance of this achievement is all the more remarkable because Americans manifest a variety of attitudes on domestic matters and hold diverse views on how U.S. foreign policy should be oriented. These views may frequently not be based on any thorough knowledge of the international environment, especially foreign cultures and history, but these views nevertheless become domestic political reality with implications not only for U.S. policymakers, but also for American allies and adversaries.

To a certain extent, almost too much is known about U.S. foreign policy thinking. The data sources—oral, written, and machine readable—are inexhaustible. In one study, to illustrate the variety of information available, Eugene R. Wittkopf combined over 200 questionnaire items into 20 scales. In turn, these scales yielded six general foreign policy attitudes that he identified as:

> Accommodation with the external world;
> Involvement with it;
> Satisfaction with U.S. policymaking institutions;
> The importance of U.S. relations with other nations;
> Foreign aid as an instrument of policy; and
> A need to reorient U.S. policy and policymaking institutions.[1]

Wittkopf's study, which is simply an example of a growing genre of foreign policy scholarship in the United States, is suggestive of a public appreciation of the complexities and subtleties of international relations.[2] It might also suggest a very confused public. But the thrust of these studies, despite the assortment of methodological tools employed, is that there is some coherence in the way the American public structures very complicated and confusing events.[3]

The way in which Americans impose coherence on the world is something European observers of the American scene do a good deal of handwringing about. Since the time of de Tocqueville, Europeans have understandably been dismayed by U.S. tendencies toward isolation. This has not, however, spared Americans from European complaints about U.S. meddlesomeness in the past decades. In a sense, then, there is concern about American behavior on a scale or dimension of isolation-involvement. This concern is not at all a European monopoly nor even a non-American monopoly. It is one of the deepest rooted, ongoing debates in the U.S. republic.

But much of the point of recent studies about U.S. foreign policy is that the isolation-involvement dimension is not adequate to capture how Americans structure the external world. There are other dimensions. Not all of them, though, are of interest here. What is of particular importance in terms of transatlantic concepts of foreign policy are perceptions of European-American differences in how publics and elites structure the world.

It is fairly obvious that there is one major criticism of American views made by Europeans. It has been suggested in numerous forums that the genuine problem of the planet lies in relationships between the developed and underdeveloped world; there is a crisis along a North-South axis. The work of

Willi Brandt and voluminous studies and statements coming out of the United Nations apropos a new world economic order bear witness to this problem.[4] It is believed that the United States betrays a major insensitivity to this axis; it is fixated by its rivalry with the second world, by its confrontation with Moscow's empire. The United States is more preoccupied with communism than it should be, and less concerned with poverty than it needs to be, some charge.

It is not easy to focus on a particular foreign policy orientation, be it either North-South or East-West. People understandably become confused when, as they look to the South, they see so many manifestations of Eastern military penetration in the form of Cuban troops, East German military advisers, and Soviet weapons. At the same time, nothing seems to capture so well the sometimes confused compass of the United States as does the lifting of the grain embargo by the Reagan administration in April 1981. President Carter imposed the embargo to punish the USSR for invading Afghanistan, one of the least developed countries (North-South orientation, possibly). Reagan lifted it, ostensibly to reward the USSR for not (yet) invading Poland (East-West orientation, possibly). Essentially, this Reagan policy may suggest that his administration is more sensitive to East-West moves on the part of the USSR than it is to North-South moves on the Soviets' behalf. While this may suit Reagan's personal ideology, it also suits at least one of several U.S. foreign policy constituencies: people who tend to give priority to the accommodation of domestic economic interests over hardline opposition to communism. Obviously, there are many foreign policy constituencies, some only temporary, others more consistent in the pursuit of their foreign policy goals. Indeed, these constituencies are likely to show considerable overlap. It is useful to take a closer look at four constituencies that have become broadly defined over a period of several years.

The basis for identifying these constituencies in public opinion flows, in part at least, from the discussion in the preceding paragraph. The themes of isolation-involvement and East-West versus North-South orientations are important. There are some very complex ways of identifying these constituencies that are still being debated. A very simple route to classify members of the public into constituencies of opinion will be used. From there, one will be able to track their relative numbers over time, examine how they structure the outside world, and analyze their policy preferences.

The data base employed here is the General Social Survey of NORC, which has been conducted regularly since a pilot study was undertaken in 1972. The great value of this study comes from the fact that the sample base is nationwide, the questions cover a wide range of topics, and questions are repeated either annually or on a rotational basis. As a result, several studies can be aggregated into a single file containing data covering most of the last decade.

Much of this set of information is useful in separating Americans into categories or constituencies according to their East-West or North-South orientation. The artifice employed here depended on answers to two questions. Respondents were asked, in East-West terms:

> Thinking about all the different kinds of governments in the world today, which of these statements comes closest to how you feel about Communism as a form of government?
> 1. It's the worst kind of all.
> 2. It's bad, but no worse than some others.
> 3. It's all right for some countries.
> 4. It's a good form of government.[5]

Those who responded that communism was the worst kind of all represent about half of the U.S. population, the half most inclined to show sensitivity to East-West perspectives on foreign policy issues.

In North-South terms, the following was selected out of a large battery of questions:

> We are faced with many problems in this country, none of which can be solved easily or inexpensively. I'm going to name some of these problems, and for each one I'd like you to tell me whether you think we're spending too much money on it, too little money, or about the right amount. . . . Are we spending too much, too little, or about the right amount on foreign aid?[6]

Across all of the years this question was asked, about 70 percent thought the United States was spending too much on foreign aid.

The rationale behind using these two questions is not unduly complicated. The first question quite obviously taps hostility to communism, which is the ideological basis of the East-West conflict. The second question, regarding foreign aid spending, is not ideological or confrontational in content, but emphasizes the kinds of economic relationships stressed by those arguing for North-South perspectives. What is being suggested here is that some Americans have one orientation or another, both, or neither.

By combining responses to these two items according to the plan presented in Figure 4.1, it is possible to label four kinds of foreign policy outlooks. The selection of labels in Figure 4.1 needs some explanation; even if they are largely borrowed from others' work, they are not quite identical in meaning. The "activist" is one who is located at the intersection of a strong East-West orientation and a strong North-South orientation—at least in terms of anticommunism and support for foreign aid programs. The "insularist" shares the activist's distaste for communism, but is not willing to spend more in poor countries. The "internationalist," like the activist, is willing to use economic tools in foreign

## Figure 4.1: A Typology of Foreign Policy Attitudes

|  |  | East-West Orientation | |
|---|---|---|---|
|  |  | *Communism worst* | *Communism less than worst* |
| Foreign Aid | Maintain or Increase | Activist | Internationalist |
|  | Spend Less | Insularist | Accommodationist |

policy, but does not structure the world in East-West terms. This is the kind of American many European elites would like to see in increasing numbers. Finally, the "accommodationist" favors a very passive role for the United States—as neither a bulwark against communism nor as a banker to finance world development.

There are some important comparisons and contrasts that can be made here just to clarify this terminology. Take for example the activist-internationalist pair. Both perceive the importance of economics-based foreign programs, but the activists are simultaneously hostile to communism. The insularist and accommodationist share a desire to cut foreign aid. But the accommodationists also express much less hostility to communism. At one extreme of orientations, consequently, one can see the activists who have both an East-West and a North-South active orientation; the accommodationists have neither.

This kind of classification approach has good and bad points. Based as it is on two variables, it suffers from a calibration difficulty. The reliability with which one can measure things is partially a function of the number of measurement points we employ. On the other hand, there are few clear foreign policy concepts that can be defined, much less measured. But a pair of exceptions are attitudes toward communism and foreign aid.

One should now ask how many of each type of constituency exist. Table 4.1 serves as a point of departure for this issue. The information in this table needs comment in two areas. The first concerns the relative sizes of the various constituencies. Over time, the two largest groups (accounting between them for roughly 75 percent of the public) have been the insularists and accommodationists. But the balance between them has been changing. The insularist group has shown an almost unbroken tendency to increase; the

## TABLE 4.1: Distribution of Foreign Policy Constituency Types, 1973 to 1980 (percent)

| Type | 1973 | 1974 | 1976 | 1977 | 1980 |
|---|---|---|---|---|---|
| Activist | 10.2 | 10.2 | 11.0 | 15.1 | 12.8 |
| Insularist | 33.9 | 40.2 | 41.3 | 38.9 | 45.1 |
| Internationalist | 15.4 | 11.0 | 10.7 | 13.9 | 13.5 |
| Accommodationist | 40.5 | 38.6 | 37.1 | 32.1 | 28.6 |
| N | 1,379 | 1,385 | 1,405 | 1,401 | 1,360 |

Source: Computed by authors from NORC General Social Survey 1972-80 Combined File.

accommodationist sentiment is down to about three-quarters of what it was in 1973. This is suggestive of the demise of the post-Vietnam syndrome. Insularist sentiment, one of the long-term themes in American public opinion, jumped notably in 1974 and again in 1980. In both cases it is easy to guess why. Withdrawal behind our oceans is an instinctive American response to foreign policy reverses. Vietnam in 1974 and Iran in 1980 were certainly viewed as reverses. The smaller constituencies, the activists and the internationalists, show very little change across time; their fluctuations are not suggestive of any trends.

The background differences among the various constituency groups are not strikingly impressive. Still, there are signs of change that merit some mention. For example, in 1973 the poll evidence suggests that a majority of the college educated (54 percent) were classified in the accommodationist category; only 7 percent of the college educated placed in the activist category. By 1980 only one-third of the college educated were found to be accommodationists, while 17 percent were now in the activist category. The insularist category also received quite an infusion of educated elites. About 13 percent of college graduates were insularists in 1973. By 1980 the figure had grown to 26 percent.

Illustrating the relationship between education and classification into a foreign policy constituency would be a tedious task, involving more than 140 individual cells. On the other hand, summarizing overall relationships across the years is a much more compact effort. If one chooses a convenient and appropriate statistic such as the chi-square-based Cramer's V, the pattern of associations across the years appears as shown in Table 4.2. This set of correlations is not particularly impressive. Moreover, the trend, insofar as one appears, is toward a weakening relationship between education and foreign policy perspective.

While education, as a summary of many cultural and economic aspects of personality, may not be well related to foreign policy orientation, political affiliation as a summary of personal philosophy is even less strongly related. The statistics employed in Table 4.2 have been applied to partisanship, with

**TABLE 4.2: The Relationship between Education and Foreign Policy Constituency Groups**

| Year | Value of Cramer's V |
|------|---------------------|
| 1973 | 0.16 |
| 1974 | 0.11 |
| 1976 | 0.15 |
| 1977 | 0.13 |
| 1980 | 0.12 |

*Source*: Computed by authors from NORC General Social Survey 1972-80. Education was categorized as "Less than High School, High School Graduate, Junior College, College, and Graduate."

**TABLE 4.3: The Relationship between Partisanship and Foreign Policy Constituency Groups**

| Year | Value of Cramer's V |
|------|---------------------|
| 1973 | 0.06 |
| 1974 | 0.10 |
| 1976 | 0.10 |
| 1977 | 0.11 |
| 1978 | 0.07 |

*Source*: Computed by authors from NORC General Social Survey 1972-80. Party identification was coded as "Democrat," "Independent," and "Republican."

the results shown in Table 4.3. What these figures suggest is that foreign policy attitudes do not easily fit into elite-mass or left-right categories. To a large extent, U.S. foreign policy constituencies, at least at a general level, are not mere extensions of domestic constituencies. What, then, does separate these constituencies?

A likely place to start is to distinguish how constituencies view the outside world in terms of likes and dislikes—what social psychologists call "affect." In the polls employed here, respondents were asked over several years to rate on a scale (− 5 through + 5) a series of countries, including the Soviet Union, Japan, Great Britain, Canada, Brazil, the People's Republic of China, Israel, and Egypt* as to how much they liked these countries. This

---

*Country names were popularized, that is, "Russia" and "China" were used instead of "Soviet Union" or "People's Republic of China."

collection of countries may appear random, but it includes representation of the free world, the communist cluster, and the third world. All the countries are ones that most Americans recognize or of which they are likely to have an image.

As can be seen from Figure 4.2, the various foreign policy groups had some marked similarities. It is obvious that there were no appreciable differences among them in terms of very favorable views Americans have toward Canada and Britain. For all groups, the least-liked nation was the Soviet Union. However, the insularists and activists were considerably more inclined than the internationalists or accommodationists to dislike it. The People's Republic of China showed up nearly as unpopular as the Soviet Union, but it had relatively greater success with accommodationsts, internationalists, and activists. It is the insularists who hold China in the lowest esteem.

Between the extremes of like and dislike (Canada-Britain, Soviet Union-China), there are some nations that Americans generally like, but with reservations not extended to the favored Anglo-Saxon democracies. These include Japan, Brazil, Israel, and Egypt. In terms of average rates of approval (about +2 on the NORC scale, compared with +4.5 for Canada or −1.5 for the Soviet Union), there is very little to differentiate these countries. But the views of the separate foreign policy constituencies toward the "in-between" nations are suggestive of how different American constituencies view the world. For

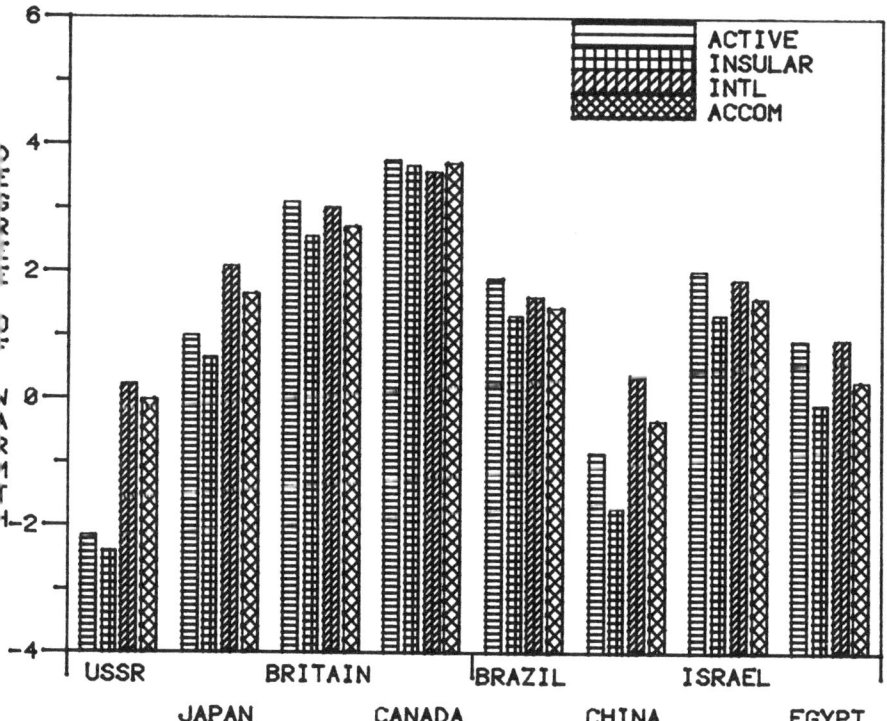

FIGURE 4.2: Feelings about Other Nations

example, the internationalists are somewhat more oriented toward the Japanese than any other group, while the insularists verge on disliking the Japanese. Essentially, the overall mean for the Japanese in terms of like-dislike is artificial. The American public is simply not of one mind regarding them. This is very understandable regarding the Japanese, and probably a widespread phenomenon from one nation to another.

Israel is another country about which Americans have not made up their minds. As was the case with Japan, Americans insularists view Israel with relative suspicion. Accommodationists are only slightly more inclined to like Israel. On the other hand, Israel is more favorably viewed by activists. There is a similar but more pronounced pattern for Egypt: insularists and accommodationists are less inclined to like it and internationalists are markedly more sanguine in outlook.

Brazil occupies a unique place among the moderately popular nations in that across the various foreign policy constituencies, there is relatively little difference save for its slightly greater popularity among the activists. This suggests, in the context of what is known about Japan, Israel, and Egypt, some modest proposals about how Americans structure the world. One obvious point is that Americans do separate their friends and enemies in a consensus pattern. Canadians and Britons are well liked; the Soviets are disliked.

A second point that needs further analysis is suggested by the views of Americans toward the other countries examined. It is not coincidental that activists are more inclined to like both Egypt and Israel. Both of these countries are (rightly) seen as aligned against the United States' chief adversary. Activists may see Brazil, as well, as playing a similar role in an East-West conflict in a remote South American context. Americans are aware of Brazil's status as a nearly developed country with a regime hardly sympathetic to Moscow.

This overview of selected countries certainly supports notions of a strong East-West consciousness on the part of the American public. But this does not mean that Americans view every nation in terms of its relationship to the USSR. At the same time, there does not seem to be any evidence that Americans (at least large numbers of them) completely reject an East-West perspective. There may be some Americans obsessed with the Soviet Union to the exclusion of the third world, but there are no signs of Americans obsessed with the third world who forget the Soviet Union. Thus while it is possible to exaggerate the American East-West orientation, it is still the underlying aspect of U.S. foreign policy thinking among the elements of the mass public.

**COMMITMENT TO DEFENSE**

To explore the strength of the East-West orientation on the part of the American public, the degree of its commitment to defense was examined.

After all, support of the military establishment is a meaningful foreign policy attitude since war, in Clausewitzian terms, is the ultimate extension of foreign policy.[7]

Probably the most meaningful way to probe feelings about a particular issue is to attach a cost to it and ask Americans if they would be willing to pay more for it. This approach was used earlier in this chapter with foreign aid and found a less-than-enthusiastic public. When a similar question about the military, armaments, and defense was put to the public (are we spending too much, about the right amount, too little?), the results provided an interesting commentary on the evolution of spending priorities among the people of the United States. Figure 4.3 shows a steady increase from 1973 to 1980 of those who wish to spend more on the military forces and armaments, and thereby express a greater commitment. A similar, but less dramatic, increase in spending is also manifested for space exploration, which obviously has favorable implications for defense as well. On the other hand, beginning with 1975, Figure 4.3 shows a gradual but steady decline of those who believe that too little is spent on welfare. A breakdown of the increase in spending priorities for defense by the four foreign policy constituencies is shown in Figure 4.4. Note that the insularists show the highest support trend while that of the internationalists is lowest.

The surveys taken by the Gallup Organization for the CCFR in 1974 and 1978 show a similar rise in American commitment to defense. In 1974 13 percent of the respondents thought that the United States was spending too little on the military, but in 1978 that figure was 32 percent.

What do those supporting increased defense spending have in mind as to its utilization? In the CCFR study, a series of hypothetical questions was posed—questions depicting situations that might call for the use of U.S. troops. Among these 11 hypothetical situations were included a Soviet invasion of Yugoslavia, a Cuban invasion of Rhodesia, and an Arab cutoff of oil to the United States. Only two situations elicited major public support for the use of troops: a Panamanian closure of the canal to U.S. ships (58 percent) and a Soviet invasion of Western Europe (54 percent). By contrast, only 22 percent would use troops to defend Israel from an Arab invasion.[8] In effect, then, the status of U.S. opinion prior to the Iranian crisis was one of increased support for defense spending and a willingness to use it for resolving threats close to home (Panama) and away from home (Europe). Thus one sees a reluctance to make specific commitments for the use of U.S. forces everywhere, but a greater willingness to honor such commitments in particular crucial areas.[9]

This implications this figure (4.4) and the information it contains have for the often discussed post-Vietnam syndrome should be examined. For example, in 1973 even the most bellicose foreign policy constituency identified—the insularists—contained less than 20 percent who said the United States should spend more on arms. Fewer than 10 percent of the accommodationists thought more should be spent.

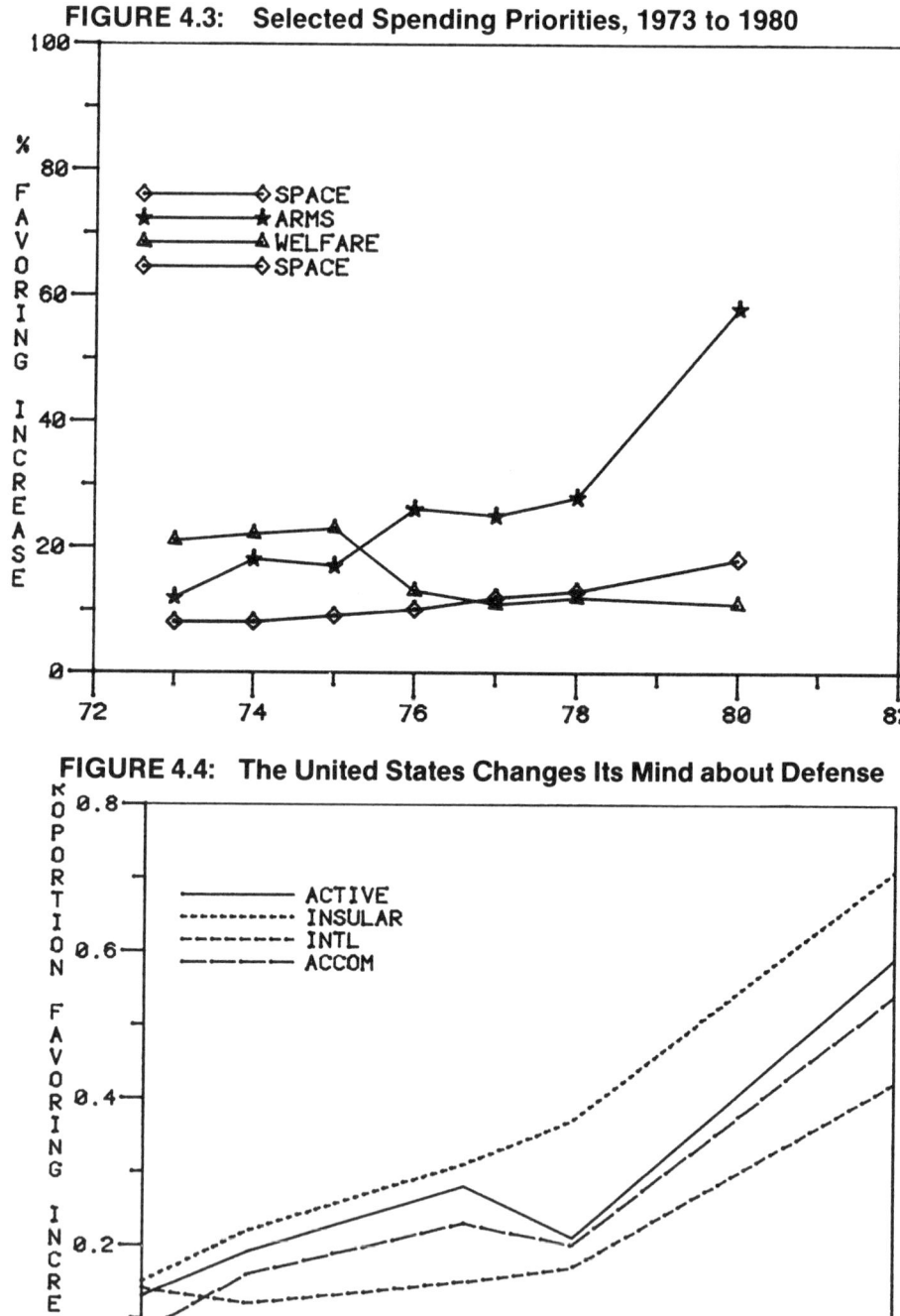

FIGURE 4.3: Selected Spending Priorities, 1973 to 1980

FIGURE 4.4: The United States Changes Its Mind about Defense

By the time Carter was inaugurated (1977), defense consciousness among the insularists was beginning to make them quite distinguishable from the other groups who had only slightly moved from their 1973 positions. But by the end of the Carter years (1980), all groups had greatly increased support for defense spending. There is a certain irony here, given Carter's steadfast pursuit of detente. It is tempting to suggest that Carter's policies were undone by Iran— just as perhaps Carter was. But as the hostages fade into their jobs, Iran has faded from American consciousness. What remains in the American consciousness as the Reagan years open is an awareness of the USSR's threat, and widespread acknowledgement of the plausibility of the Reagan administration's claim that detente can be pursued earnestly only after the United States arms itself further.

What effect does age have on the respondent's spending priorities? There have been assertions that the so-called Vietnam generation, those born between 1943 and 1954, might espouse different values than the generation preceding it because of the experiences its members encountered during the Vietnam war.[10] Hence, it has been claimed, the attitudes of that age group remain different even today.

Whatever attitudes the Vietnam generation may have had earlier, they have converged gradually with the attitudes of both the post-Vietnam and pre-Vietnam generations. This can be seen in Figure 4.5, which shows the average percentage support for spending increases for arms, environment, foreign aid, and welfare by the three generational groups. As far as support for arms is concerned, the pre-Vietnam group shows the highest percentage, but the Vietnam generation is not far below the average (21 percent). Regarding increases in spending on welfare, the Vietnam generation is right in the middle, but again the differences are not significant; here one should remember that, according to Figure 4.3, the percentage of those supporting a rise in welfare expenditures has been declining steadily. Finally, the differences between the three generations on spending for foreign aid and space exploration are also insignificant.

Another thing that bears attention in looking at the past decade's developments in American military consciousness is the rapidity and volume of change. One can choose from a wide variety of items in order to make comparisons with military spending, as was done in Figure 4.3. In Figure 4.6, additional information is presented to tell more about the context in which military spending finds itself.

Throughout the 1970s there was a strong public commitment to environmental issues and to the United States' chronic problems with crime. Crime still is the area that Americans are most willing to spend money on. Whether or not money solves the problem is less important than the symbolic nature of willingness to direct resources at the problem. The environment is also a crucial area, but Americans have, in fact, seen environmental gains. Some of the atmosphere of crisis (common in early 1970s) has passed, aided by the

78 / NATO AND THE ATLANTIC DEFENSE

**FIGURE 4.5: The Generations and Spending Priorities**

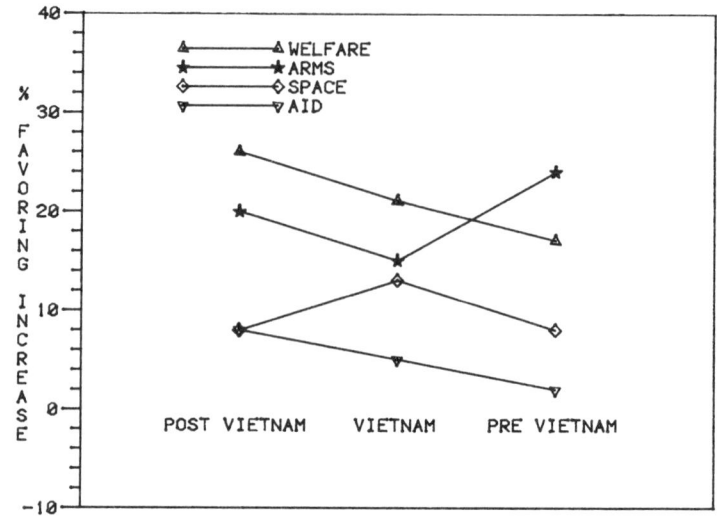

Source: 1972-80 NORC General Social Survey.

**FIGURE 4.6: Selected Spending Priorities, 1973 to 1980**

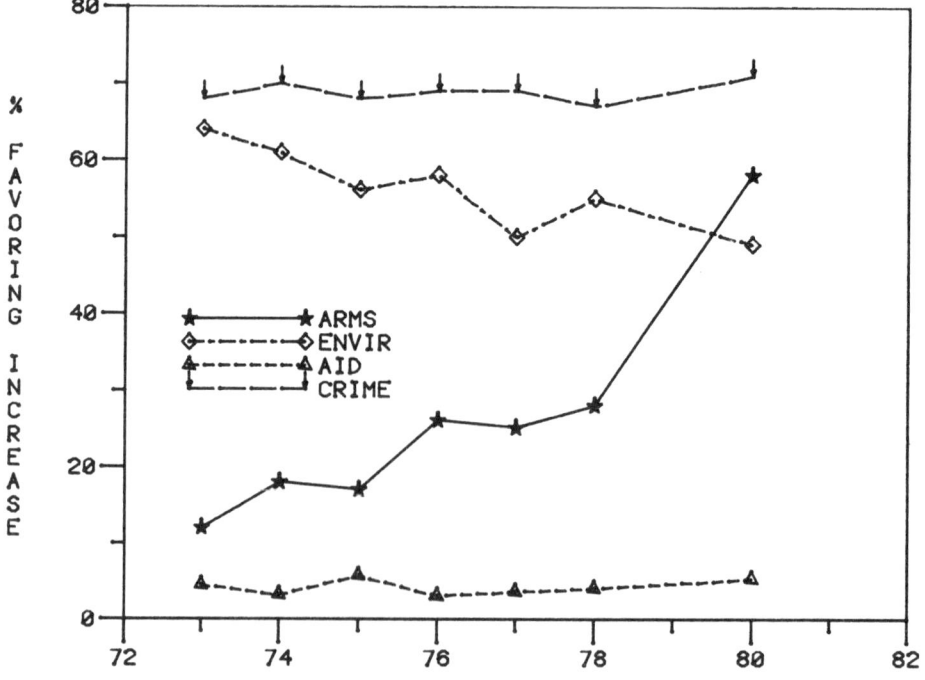

difficult choices posed by the energy crisis. Military spending, as a spending priority, has now exceeded the environment and is approaching crime in funding support.

One should not take the proportions and percentages uncovered in poll data literally. But even a short visit to the United States will convince a foreigner of the depth of concern in this country with crime. The expression of willingness to bring arms spending to the same level as crime spending is strong evidence of a major reorientation of American public opinion. So great has been the change across time that one might not pick up the evidence in the polls that defense spending is still a debatable issue among the members of the public. It is true that overall only about 12 percent of the entire public in 1973 wanted to spend more on arms; by 1980 it was 61 percent. But the very important internationalist group lagged far behind the rest of the public (see Figure 4.4). To a large extent, this group, which is not particularly worried about communism but is favorable to foreign aid, is the United States' most North-South-oriented foreign policy constituency. Leaders of this group can be expected to articulate their views and their suspicion of arms.

Europeans can take comfort from all of this. While they may not, in all quarters, appreciate the sway of East-West orientations in the United States, they should find this to their immediate advantage. After all, if the United States were really to adopt a less militant attitude toward the USSR and divert defense monies to the third world, it is quite conceivable that Europeans might be complaining about U.S. obsessions with Africa, Asia, or Latin America. It is just possible that it is the U.S. orientation toward an East-West view of the world that makes it safe for Europeans to pursue North-South strategies.

## COMMITMENT TO NATO

So far, this volume has discussed U.S. commitment to defense, the trend to increasing support for greater spending on military armaments, and the position of particular foreign policy constituencies. But what is the support of the mass public to NATO? It too has been faring well. In both 1974 and 1978, respondents were asked about the U.S. commitment to NATO: Should it be increased, kept the same, decreased, or withdrawn? Table 4.4 summarizes the changes from 1974 to 1978. What emerges is a portrait of a more defense-minded United States, with commitment to Europe and NATO on the upswing.

Indeed, another attitude survey taken by the Gallup Organization in 1980 for the Atlantic Council suggests a substantial jump of those who want to increase the U.S. commitment to NATO (21.4 percent), while only 7.1 percent wish to decrease such a commitment, and 8.3 percent want the United States to withdraw from NATO entirely (Table 4.5). These responses, elicited in a telephone survey rather than in personal interviews as in the 1974

## TABLE 4.4: Changes in U.S. Feelings toward NATO: A Growing Commitment (percent)

With regard to its commitment to NATO, the United States should:

|            | 1974 | 1978 |
|------------|------|------|
| Increase   | 4    | 9    |
| Keep same  | 51   | 59   |
| Decrease   | 13   | 9    |
| Withdraw   | 7    | NA   |

Source: Computed by authors from 1974 survey tapes and adapted from American Public Opinion and U.S. Foreign Policy, 1979.

and 1978 surveys, were made to the following question using an overall sample of 1,106 with a weighted basis of 1,525.

> Some people think that NATO, the military organization of Western Europe and the United States, has outlived its usefulness, and that the United States should withdraw militarily from NATO. Others say that NATO has discouraged the Russians from trying a military takeover in Western Europe. Do you feel we should increase our commitment to NATO, keep our commitment what it is now, decrease our commitment but still remain in NATO, or withdraw from NATO entirely?
> 1. Increase commitment
> 2. Keep commitment what it is
> 3. Decrease our commitment
> 4. Withdraw entirely
> 5. Not sure

Table 4.5 also confirms earlier indications that the impact of the successor generation on foreign policy issues has been vanishing. The youngest age group (18-29) shows the greatest desire to increase commitment to NATO, and the percentage then declines gradually to 10.2 percent of the 65-and-older age group. This suggests that the older group (from 50 to over 65), many of whom experienced World War II and are frequently assumed to be the strongest supporters of a viable defense because they are seen as the chief guardians of traditional American values, actually display the lowest interest in a stronger NATO. On the other hand, both the youngest and oldest groups are in the forefront of those wishing to decrease U.S. commitments to NATO, although the percentages are lower than those opting for an increased commitment (28.2 versus 10.4 percent and 10.2 versus 8.3 percent respectively). In terms of complete withdrawal from NATO, the 50-64 age group is the highest of all age groups. Perhaps the effect of their World War II experiences has inclined

**TABLE 4.5: The U.S. Commitment to NATO**

| | Weighted Base-Total Sample | Age | | | | Education | | | Region | | | |
|---|---|---|---|---|---|---|---|---|---|---|---|---|
| | | 18-29 | 30-49 | 50-64 | 65 & older | College | High School | Grade School | East | Mid-West | South | West |
| **Weighted base-total sample** | | | | | | | | | | | | |
| Number | 1,525 | 412 | 556 | 316 | 203 | 542 | 687 | 288 | 413 | 444 | 413 | 255 |
| Percent | 100 | 100 | 100 | 100 | 100 | 100 | 100 | 100 | 100 | 100 | 100 | 100 |
| **Commitment to NATO** | | | | | | | | | | | | |
| *Increase commitment* | | | | | | | | | | | | |
| Number | 326 | 116 | 133 | 54 | 21 | 125 | 156 | 43 | 107 | 98 | 75 | 46 |
| Percent | 21.4 | 28.2 | 23.9 | 17.1 | 10.2 | 23.1 | 22.7 | 14.9 | 25.9 | 22.1 | 18.2 | 18.0 |
| *Keep commitment what it is* | | | | | | | | | | | | |
| Number | 665 | 164 | 265 | 139 | 79 | 271 | 297 | 94 | 169 | 205 | 166 | 125 |
| Percent | 43.6 | 39.8 | 47.7 | 44.0 | 39.5 | 50.0 | 43.2 | 32.6 | 40.9 | 46.2 | 40.2 | 49.0 |
| *Decrease commitment* | | | | | | | | | | | | |
| Number | 109 | 43 | 32 | 16 | 17 | 44 | 45 | 19 | 41 | 25 | 29 | 14 |
| Percent | 7.1 | 10.4 | 5.8 | 5.1 | 8.3 | 8.1 | 6.6 | 6.6 | 9.9 | 5.6 | 7.0 | 5.5 |
| *Withdraw entirely* | | | | | | | | | | | | |
| Number | 126 | 27 | 38 | 41 | 14 | 35 | 57 | 33 | 29 | 33 | 39 | 25 |
| Percent | 8.3 | 6.6 | 6.8 | 13.0 | 6.8 | 6.5 | 8.3 | 11.5 | 7.0 | 7.4 | 9.4 | 9.8 |
| *Not sure* | | | | | | | | | | | | |
| Number | 299 | 62 | 88 | 66 | 74 | 67 | 132 | 99 | 67 | 83 | 104 | 45 |
| Percent | 19.6 | 15.0 | 15.8 | 20.9 | 36.1 | 12.4 | 19.2 | 34.4 | 16.2 | 18.7 | 23.2 | 17.6 |

*Source:* Gallup Organization, Inc., Questions 3-5 OU 924/825B; October 1980.

them toward a more insular/isolationist orientation rather than an internationalist/activist tendency.

Table 4.5 also provides information about the influence of the educational level on the responses to the question asked. The higher the level of education of the respondents, the greater is their support of the United States' commitment to NATO.

Finally, Table 4.5 offers a regional breakdown of the responses. The East and Midwest show the greatest support for an increased commitment; the West is lowest, perhaps again a reflection of the phenomenon apparent in the discussion in Chapter 2, whereby physical distance from Europe has an influence on concerns about and interest in particular foreign events. Nevertheless, even the West does not want to decrease or withdraw the U.S. commitment to NATO. The other regional data are not sufficiently clear-cut to draw general conclusions.

A second interesting question posed in the Gallup interviews was the following:

> I am going to read you a list of countries. For each please tell me whether you feel the U.S. should or should not come to the aid of this country with military force if attacked by the Soviet Union.

The countries listed were Canada, France, England, Japan, Saudi Arabia, Israel, and Turkey. Table 4.6 furnishes the answers. Canada and England fared especially well as respectively 86.8 and 75.9 percent of the respondents opted for the employment of military force to aid these countries in the event of a Soviet attack. Obviously, this is evidence of the Anglo-Saxon "connection" at work. Support for militarily aiding France, an old ally of the United States,

**TABLE 4.6: The Use of Military Force in the Event of Soviet Intervention**

|  | Should | | Should Not | | Don't Know | |
| --- | --- | --- | --- | --- | --- | --- |
|  | Number | Percent | Number | Percent | Number | Percent |
| Canada | 1,323 | 86.8 | 80 | 5.2 | 122 | 8.0 |
| France | 913 | 59.9 | 327 | 21.4 | 295 | 18.7 |
| England | 1,157 | 75.9 | 176 | 11.5 | 192 | 12.6 |
| Japan | 871 | 57.1 | 394 | 25.8 | 260 | 17.0 |
| Saudi Arabia | 686 | 45.0 | 558 | 36.6 | 281 | 18.4 |
| Israel | 842 | 55.2 | 457 | 30.0 | 226 | 14.8 |
| Turkey | 551 | 36.1 | 619 | 40.6 | 355 | 23.3 |

Base total sample: 1,525
Number of interviews: 1,016

is substantially lower (59.9 percent). For Israel, whose security has been officially proclaimed by the U.S. government as a matter of high priority, it is still lower (55.2 percent). The use of military force for Japan is advocated by surprisingly large numbers of respondents (57.1 percent) considering the shades of trade wars overhanging the U.S.-Japanese relationship and recurring frictions about the shape of the military ties. Only a strong minority (45 percent) supports military involvement to aid Saudi Arabia in spite of the obvious adverse effects on the U.S. economy if that country were to be a victim of a Soviet attack. Military support for Turkey in the event of such an attack is voiced by an even smaller number of the respondents (36.1 percent).

A few comments are in order regarding the influence of age, education, and region of the respondents. Those aged 30-49 years are the strongest advocates for the employment of military force for all seven countries. This is another piece of evidence that the Vietnam generation, which had particular policy preferences shaped by the Vietnam experience, has found its way again into the mainstream of U.S. attitudes regarding foreign policy. In terms of education, college graduates scored consistently higher in their support of military action to aid all countries in the event of Soviet aggression. Finally, respondents living in the West showed greater tendencies toward military action to assist other countries if attacked except Israel and Turkey, for which respondents in the South took top honors. For complete data, see Appendix C.

A third and final question in the Gallup survey deals with the Persian Gulf.

> The President [Carter] has said in his State of the Union message: "An attempt by an outside force to gain control of the Persian Gulf region will be regarded as an assault on the vital interest of the U.S. It will be repelled by use of any means necessary, including military force."
>
> Would you say you would agree strongly, agree, disagree, or disagree strongly with this policy?

Table 4.7 shows that a substantial majority "strongly agrees" or "agrees" with the policy pronounced by President Carter. But about one in four of the respondents disagrees. Again, the two youngest age groups (18-29 and 30-49) are the most supportive of this policy and the college graduates lead the less educated. In terms of regional distribution, respondents living in the East are the most enthusiastic backers of the Carter stand.

Taken together with the increasing commitment to NATO and the rising defense consciousness of the American people, the data demonstrate a growing willingness of the public to assert vital U.S. interests in the world, even if it were necessary to employ armed forces. It is noteworthy and significant that

## TABLE 4.7: The Defense of the Persian Gulf Region

Q.5 Do you agree/disagree with President Carter's statement of military force if the Persian Gulf region was attacked?

| | Weighted Base-Total Sample | Age | | | | | Education | | | Region | | | |
|---|---|---|---|---|---|---|---|---|---|---|---|---|---|
| | | 18-29 | 30-49 | 50-64 | 65 & older | | Col-lege | High School | Grade School | East | Mid-West | South | West |
| **Weighted base-total sample** | | | | | | | | | | | | | |
| Number | 1,525 | 412 | 556 | 316 | 205 | | 542 | 687 | 288 | 413 | 444 | 413 | 255 |
| Percent | 100 | 100 | 100 | 100 | 100 | | 100 | 100 | 100 | 100 | 100 | 100 | 100 |
| **Agree/Disagree** | | | | | | | | | | | | | |
| Agree strongly | | | | | | | | | | | | | |
| Number | 313 | 77 | 124 | 71 | 33 | | 123 | 142 | 47 | 86 | 71 | 103 | 53 |
| Percent | 20.5 | 18.7 | 22.3 | 22.5 | 16.1 | | 22.7 | 20.7 | 16.3 | 20.8 | 16.0 | 24.9 | 20.8 |
| Agree | | | | | | | | | | | | | |
| Number | 590 | 189 | 245 | 82 | 61 | | 236 | 262 | 88 | 180 | 173 | 138 | 99 |
| Percent | 38.7 | 45.9 | 44.1 | 25.9 | 29.8 | | 43.5 | 38.1 | 30.6 | 43.6 | 39.0 | 33.4 | 38.8 |
| Disagree | | | | | | | | | | | | | |
| Number | 328 | 105 | 107 | 69 | 40 | | 108 | 153 | 66 | 75 | 113 | 87 | 53 |
| Percent | 21.5 | 25.5 | 19.2 | 21.8 | 19.5 | | 19.9 | 22.3 | 22.9 | 18.2 | 25.5 | 21.1 | 20.8 |
| Disagree strongly | | | | | | | | | | | | | |
| Number | 71 | 20 | 31 | 15 | 4 | | 31 | 32 | 7 | 22 | 23 | 18 | 9 |
| Percent | 4.7 | 4.9 | 5.6 | 4.7 | 2.0 | | 5.7 | 4.7 | 2.4 | 5.3 | 5.2 | 4.1 | 3.5 |
| Don't know | | | | | | | | | | | | | |
| Number | 223 | 21 | 49 | 79 | 67 | | 44 | 98 | 80 | 50 | 64 | 68 | 41 |
| Percent | 14.6 | 5.1 | 8.8 | 25.0 | 32.7 | | 8.1 | 14.3 | 27.8 | 12.1 | 14.4 | 16.5 | 16.1 |

Source: Gallup Organization, Inc., Questions 3-5 on 824/825P; October 1980.

the younger generations are in the forefront of this trend. Indeed, this trend, as shown by an examination of nationwide data, is confirmed by the authors' survey of student attitudes at the University of New Orleans in fall 1979. Over 80 percent of the respondents expressed the view that without NATO the United States would be weaker, and that NATO helps protect the American way of life.[11]

## THE ROLE OF THE MEDIA

What is the role of the media in the formation of attitudes about NATO and defense in general? Chapter 1 examined the public image of NATO; here the inquiry is broadened to include readership and television viewers' interest in foreign news and its effect on attitude development.

Table 4.8 shows that the role of the press is ambiguous. Here the question reads:

> When you pick up a newspaper these days, how interested are you in reading articles relating to news about other countries?

When this question was crosstabulated with feelings about NATO, and specifically with a decrease of support for NATO, the figures in Table 4.8 emerge. The degree of association in this table is not strong, but what is suggested is that the "attentive public" is polarized: the greater the level of interest the greater *and* lesser the degree of support. In effect, interest decreases the "not sure" responses more than it increases support.

On the other hand, there is evidence of change. Remember, Table 4.8 was drawn from 1974 data. Using 1977 data on a question about television, one finds quite different results. Here, the questions relate feelings about

**TABLE 4.8: The Ambiguous Role of the Media I: Interest in Foreign News in the Press and Commitment to NATO (percent)**

| The U.S. should | Very Interested | Somewhat Interested | Hardly Interested |
|---|---|---|---|
| Withdraw or decrease | 31 | 21 | 19 |
| Not sure | 20 | 23 | 31 |
| Keep same or increase | 59 | 56 | 50 |
| Total | 100 | 100 | 100 |
| N | 502 | 597 | 293 |

Source: CCFR 1974 Survey provided by Interuniversity Consortium for Political and Social Research.

defense spending to hours of television watched, grouped into "low" and "high." The somewhat clearer pattern of Table 4.9, more television producing sympathy for defense spending, may be affected somewhat by differences between the "press informed" and the "video informed." But it is strongly suspected that Table 4.9 captures, as well, an ongoing change in U.S. public opinion: the more informed are more defense conscious compared with a few years ago. In effect, the public may be leading the media.

One source that is helpful in examining this notion is the Foreign Policy Association's "Great Decisions" program. One of the 1979 topics was "NATO and the Russians: Will the East-West Balance Hold?" The 5,120 ballot forms returned on this topic are hardly representative of a cross section of the U.S. public. Rather, they represent a self-selected attentive public who has expressed extraordinary interest in foreign policy problems. An examination of their ballot patterns shows that the participants place their highest hopes in "concluding agreements with the Soviet Union that would lead to a reduction of military forces on both sides in Europe." In 1979, 53 percent of the participants suggested that this be a first priority; in a sense, they are strongly behind mutual balanced reduction of forces, a familiar NATO policy. The second favored alternative (40 percent) is putting first priority status on "strengthening NATO." Actually, both policies strengthen NATO, but the second policy alternative applies explicitly to equipment and troops. Moreover, the ballots indicate that the participants are aware of the costs of defending Europe from the Soviets and that they are willing to bear some sacrifice to pay for that defense. Thus there is strong evidence that the attentive public is aware of the need for defense and the cost as well. This is quite at variance with the thesis of a genre of media treatment of arms policy typified by the CBS production "The Selling of the Pentagon," one of the most controversial antimilitary documentaries to follow the Vietnam war.

Indeed, there is a history of latent media hostility to the military in the past few years—or at least charges of that hostility backed up with some note-

**TABLE 4.9: The Ambiguous Role of the Media II: Hours of TV Exposure and Feelings about Defense Spending (percent)**

| The U.S. spends | Hours of TV Exposure | |
|---|---|---|
| | Low | High |
| Too little | 24 | 28 |
| About right | 48 | 50 |
| Too much | 28 | 22 |
| Total | 100 | 100 |
| N | 708 | 692 |

Source: NORC 1977 General Social Survey provided by ICPSR.

worthy evidence. This may be why some of the evidence presented is ambiguous. But as for now, the latest evidence is that media exposure or attention is correlated with, though not the sole cause of, increased support for a defense effort. This evidence comes from the 1978 Chicago Council on Foreign Relations poll. CCFR's approach is to divide the public into levels of attentiveness. Table 4.10 shows the relationship found in its 1978 survey between these levels of attentiveness and support of expanded defense spending. This table is very convincing evidence of what the media's impact is now. One is not sure, though, what the direction of causality is, or even the nature of it. The previous sections dealing with media content show generally sympathetic media in terms of editorial content. They also show the media reacting to newsworthy events that, without editorial frills, are quite sufficient to worry the American public about its defense posture. The public is aware of the Soviet arms buildup. It may be that the media are responding to the public instead of the other way around.

Even with the present reservations about causality, it is increasingly obvious that the United States is in the process of reversing its policy of maximum armament restraint that followed the Vietnam debacle. This phenomenon, however, has both short- and long-term causes. The long-term causes, events that can be grouped under the label of "Soviet expansionism," clearly work to NATO's interest. Short-term causes include the rapid installation of SS-20 missiles in Europe by the Soviet Union and, most recently, the Afghanistan invasion. These events have led to greater U.S. assertiveness vis-à-vis the Soviets in Europe. Certainly, the U.S. decision to press for deployment of the Pershing missile weapons system in Europe is a sign of a stiffening of attitudes. The pursuit of detente must be backed up by a balance of weapons and forces in the European theater.

### SUMMARY AND CONCLUSIONS

What conclusions can be drawn from the examination and analysis in Chapters 2 and 3 of the NATO image projected in the United States, trends

**TABLE 4.10: Public Attentiveness and Percent Wanting to Expand Defense Spending: The Impact of the Media**

|  | Public Attentiveness | | |
| --- | --- | --- | --- |
|  | Low | Medium | High |
| Percent who want to expand defense spending | 19 | 34 | 52 |

Source: CCFR, American Public Opinion and U.S. Foreign Policy 1979, p. 25.

in American public opinion regarding defense and NATO, and the possible interaction between the NATO image and public opinion in the United States?

First, the public image (as noted in Chapter 2) is generally favorable and is bolstered by a public opinion which, during the last few years, has become increasingly defense conscious and now gives a very high priority to the protection of Western Europe against a Soviet attack. This has occurred simultaneously with greater backing for defense-related expenditures at the expense of social welfare items. However, this does not mean that support for NATO and Atlantic defense is unconditional. The American public and elites are especially sensitive to possible manifestations of lagging financial and political cooperation in NATO. The very recent reluctance of Belgium and and the Netherlands to accept nuclear theater weapons for deployment in the early 1980s has produced a measure of consternation among the attentive public.

Second, the favorable inclination of the public toward NATO may well be in part the result of media exposure. But there is also a direct relationship between willingness to spend money on defense and the respondents' support of NATO. Moreover, the data suggest that the public largely views NATO as synonymous with defense, as increased commitment to higher spending for defense appears to go hand-in-hand with increased commitment to NATO.

Third, Europeans should not focus exclusively on the current U.S. consensus to build a stronger defense force. Armament is not a substitute for foreign policy—a point that is quite well understood in the United States. At the present time, the policy behind U.S. defense expenditures is based largely on an East-West perspective of international affairs. This perspective is not based on perversity nor on indifference to North-South problems; it is based on the realization that 20 years of expanded Soviet arms procurement has weakened the United States and threatens to bring about the neutralization of Europe. Indeed, U.S. strategic defenses seem to be in such disrepair that only one leg of the nuclear triad—submarines—is not faced with immediate obsolescence.

Still, as the United States regains strategic equality with the Soviet Union, options will present themselves in the area of foreign policy orientation—and there are Americans willing to pursue those options, as this chapter's identification of various foreign policy constituencies suggests. Furthermore, even within the Reagan administration there is a variety of views. Secretary of State Haig is an obvious East-West-oriented person, but with a sensitivity to North-South issues. In the authors' terms, he would be an "activist." Defense Secretary Weinberger and National Security Advisor Allen are in the insularist tradition. They are hardly sentimental about the United States' ties with Europe; they are likely to tolerate, albeit very grudgingly, a Finlandized or neutralized Europe provided U.S. military strength would be sufficient to assure this country's access to strategic materials throughout the world.

Most Americans, for the time being (even the insularists and accommodationists), are still fairly sentimentally committed to NATO. There is a lot of "affect" in American public opinion. Of course, most of that affect is directed toward neighboring Canada and cultural cousin Britain. But as the poll data presented here demonstrate, many Americans would be willing to fight to defend allies as diverse as France, Israel, and Japan should they be attacked by the Soviet Union. On the other hand, it is very unlikely that Americans will unduly interfere with allies who want to neutralize themselves and abandon themselves to Soviet protection. Some Americans and Europeans think that the process of neutralization is already well advanced. This is the topic of the following chapters.

## NOTES

1. Adapted from Eugene R. Wittkopf, "The Structure of Foreign Policy Attitudes: An Alternative View," *Social Science Quarterly* 62 (March 1981): 110-12.

2. Wittkopf's article is part of a methodological debate joined with views expressed by Barbara Bardes and Robert Oldendick, "Beyond Internationalism: A Case for Multiple Dimensions in the Structure of Foreign Policy Attitudes," *Social Science Quarterly* 59 (December 1978): 496-508. Bardes and Oldendick responded to Wittkopf in their "The Continuing Case for Multiple Dimensions in the Structure of Foreign Policy Attitudes," *Social Science Quarterly* 62 (March 1981): 124-27.

3. Very useful in this regard is Michael Mandelbaum and William Schneider, "The New Internationalisms," in *Eagle Entangled: U.S. Foreign Policy in a Complex World*, eds. Kenneth A. Oye, Donald Rothchild, and Robert J. Lieber (New York: Longman, 1979), pp. 34-88.

4. See also Karl Kaiser, Winston Lord, Thierry de Monthrial, and David Watt, *Western Security: What Has Changed? What Should Be Done?* (New York: Council on Foreign Relations, 1981), pp. 34-41.

5. James A. Davis, *General Social Surveys, 1972-1980: Cumulative Codebook* (Chicago: NORC, 1980), p. 84.

6. Ibid., p. 73.

7. Carl von Clausewitz was a Prussian general who devoted a great deal of his fertile thoughts to the nature of war. See his book *On War*, ed. and trans. Michael Howard and Peter Parat (Princeton, N.J.: Princeton University Press, 1976).

8. John W. Rielly, ed., *American Public Opinion and U.S. Foreign Policy 1979* (Chicago: Chicago Council on Foreign Relations, 1979), p. 26.

9. Ibid., p. 27.

10. See the Atlantic Council of the United States, *The Successor Generation* (Washington, D.C., 1981).

11. See Chapter 3 for details.

# 5

# EURODOVES AND EUROHAWKS

## SOME TECHNICAL COMMENTS

One of the greatest advantages students of U.S. public opinion have over their opposite numbers in Europe is the ease, at least in a comparative sense, with which a nationwide American sample can be drawn. To draw similar samples in Europe as a whole is a much more expensive matter than is the case in the United States. This has nothing to do with the many differences between the respective population sizes of the two continents, but, instead, to the much greater variability of the European population in terms of political opinions and cultures. For example, it is very likely that a sample of Italians and Britons will differ from each other much more markedly than would a sample of Northerners and Southerners in the United States. As a consequence of this greater European variability, it is often necessary to draw independent samples in each European nation—each one of these samples being about the size of a continentwide U.S. sample. Thus a comparison of the United States with the European communities would require, hypothetically, a 1,000 respondent sample from Americans and a 10,000 respondent sample from Europeans: 1,000 from each member state.

This prelude should serve to suggest two things about the pages that follow. Because of its great variability, European public opinion holds a great fascination for political scientists. For the same reason, the findings of political scientists cannot have the certainty they might have if expressed about opinions in the United States.

Discussion of the kinds of data available on a Europewide basis will make this clearer. The most important effort to regularly gather European (or at least Community) public opinion data is the Eurobarometer series, now semiannual, sponsored by the Commission of the European Community (EC). But until spring 1980, the Eurobarometer concentrated largely on intracommunity affairs. In 1973 it did range afield and ask various Community citizens how much trust they had in other nations—those in the EC, Switzerland, the People's Republic of China, the Soviet Union, and the United States. But from the period 1973 to 1980, there was an absense of questions pertaining to military and strategic concerns. On the other hand, Eurobarometers are unparalleled as a source of information about how Europeans see themselves as Europeans.[1]

However, if investigators want to focus more narrowly on strategic themes, it is necessary to turn to data gathered in Europe by the United States International Communication Agency (USICA). This agency regularly adds questions of interest to itself to surveys taken by polling organizations for entirely different purposes, such as marketing certain household products. This kind of buying-in to a questionnaire is commonly known as "piggybacking." The practice of piggybacking has certain dangers, such as the limitation of the sample to likely consumers (underrepresenting the poor) and contamination of response by other questions in the survey. The great advantage of piggybacking is that it greatly reduces costs and thus makes possible inquiries that would not have been feasible otherwise.[2]

As a consequence, the data on hand are of very good quality and were gathered with full attention to, and knowledge of, the many things that can go wrong in gathering opinions on political subjects. When one examines USICA data, one finds their analyses to be quite different than for material coming from the Interuniversity Consortium for Political and Social Research (ICPSR). The USICA data were much more recent—barely behind the headlines—but not as readily available to the public. The path the data take is from interviewer, to polling organization, to coding, to report to the State Department, transfer of data to the National Archives, and eventual release to the public. The process is more accelerated than is usually the case at ICPSR, but there is a price to be paid in the amount of technical "cleaning" of the data and documentary support. For example, data are often received by the National Archives in multiple-punched format. This is fine for electromechanical countersorters, but it tends to baffle contemporary statistical software. In addition, polling agencies in Western Europe do not have a common standard encoding data even if they are not multiple-punched. As a result, it is necessary not only to master foreign language interview schedules, but also to unsnarl alien coding logic. Once these tasks are out of the way, the surveys can be combined into a single file and processed with conventional methods and packages.*

---

*SPSS version 8.1 and some locally prepared routines were used. Some features of SAS and OSIRIS not available in SPSS currently would have proven useful.

While several studies were available, going back to the mid to late 1970s, the most timely and rewarding surveys were taken in Britain, France, and the Federal Republic of Germany in March 1980 following the Soviet invasion of Afghanistan. Of more importance to the present study were the questions about how the populations in these countries viewed the United States and their alliance with it. Constant reference will be made to some of these questions in order to facilitate reference to the various core questions from the overall interview schedule. The questionnaire is reproduced as Exhibit 5.1.

**EXHIBIT 5.1  Multiregional Security Survey Questionnaire: West Europe**

1. (CORE) What in your opinion are the two or three most important problems facing our country at the present time? (PROBE, IF ONLY ONE: What other problems are particularly important?) (SUGGESTED PARTIAL CODE)
    Domestic problems:
    1   Inflation, cost of living
    2   Unemployment
    3   Low productivity, inefficiency
    4   Strikes
    5   Other domestic economic problems
    6   Law and order
    7   Inadequate health care, pensions, other social benefits
    8   Quality of life, overcrowding, housing, pollution
    9   Other domestic concerns
    0   No answer
    X   Don't know
    Y   Blank

    International Problems:
    1   Soviet actions in Afghanistan
    2   Increasing tensions between USSR/East and U.S./West
    3   Growth of Soviet military power/Soviet threat
    4   Common Market
    5   Energy/high cost fuel, shortages
    6   (Code not used)
    7   (Code not used)
    8   (Code not used)
    9   Other international concerns
    0   No answer
    X   Don't know
    Y   Blank

2. (CORE)   Here is a list of things some people think are problems facing the world today (HAND CARD 1). Please read over this list and tell me which *two* of these you personally think are the most serious problems for the world at the present time. (TWO ANSWERS)

   1   Arab-Israeli conflict
   2   Economic gap between rich and poor countries
   3   Soviet military action in Afghanistan
   4   High cost of oil
   5   Vietnamese military actions in Cambodia
   6   Cuban military activities in other countries
   7   Growth of Soviet military power
   8   U.S. interference in other countries' affairs
   9   Influence of multinational corporations
   0   Increasing tension between the U.S. and the USSR
   X   Don't know
   Y   No answer
   
   (CARD 1)

3. (CORE)   What country do you think is the most powerful in the world at the present time?

   1   China
   2   USSR
   3   U.S.
   4   West Germany
   5   Great Britain/United Kingdom
   6   Japan
   7   France
   8   European Community
   9   Other (specify)
   0   Don't know, undecided, no opinion
   X   No answer
   Y   Blank

4. (CORE)   And what about five years from now? What country do you think will be the most powerful in the world? (PRECODE)

   1   China
   2   USSR
   3   U.S.
   4   West Germany
   5   Great Britain/United Kingdom
   6   Japan
   7   France

8   European Community
9   Other (specify)
0   Don't know, undecided, no opinion
X   No answer
Y   Blank

5. Which one of the courses listed on this card seems to you the best way to provide for the security of our country? (HAND CARD 2)

1   The NATO (North Atlantic Treaty Organization) alliance among the countries of Western Europe and the United States
2   An independent West European defense force under European command, but allied to the United States
3   An independent West European defense force under European command, but not allied to the United States
4   Rely on our own nation's defense forces without belonging to any military alliance
5   Reduce our defense forces and rely on greater accommodation with the Soviet Union

(CARD 2)

6. Regardless of your own feelings about (COUNTRY'S) membership in NATO, do you think NATO should just provide security against a possible Soviet attack in Western Europe, or do you feel that NATO should also help protect our vital interests in other parts of the world?

1   Just provide security in Western Europe
2   Also protect vital interests elsewhere
3   Don't know
0   No answer
Y   Blank

7. Do you think that the level of (COUNTRY'S) expenditures for military purposes should be increased, decreased, or left at about their present level?

1   Increased
2   Left at about present level
3   Decreased
4   Don't know
0   No answer
X   Blank

(IF *"INCREASED"* ON Q.7)

7a. Do you think (COUNTRY) should spend more for military purposes even though taxes might go up or social services might decline as a result? Or do you think we should not increase military spending under those conditions?

- 1 Spend more even though taxes might go up
- 2 Should not increase under those conditions
- 3 Don't know
- 0 No answer
- X Blank

8. In the event our country's security were threatened by a Soviet attack, how much confidence do you feel we can have in the U.S. to come to our defense—a great deal, a fair amount, not very much, or none at all?

- 1 Great deal
- 2 Fair amount
- 3 Not very much
- 4 None at all
- 5 Don't know
- 0 No answer
- X Blank

9. Which do you think is more powerful at the present time: the West, that is the NATO countries, or the East, that is the Warsaw Pact countries?

- 1 West/NATO countries
- 2 East/Warsaw Pact countries
- 3 Both equal (VOL.)
- 4 Don't know
- 0 No answer
- X Blank

10. Which side do you think will be more powerful five years from now?

- 1 West/NATO countries
- 2 East-Warsaw Pact countries
- 3 Both equal (VOL.)
- 4 Don't know
- 0 No answer
- Y Blank

## PERCEPTIONS OF POWER:
## AT PRESENT AND IN THE FUTURE

The set of questions shown in Exhibit 5.1 is by no means as extensive as one would expect to find in a voting study or even in something like the Eurobarometer. This is understandable since foreign policy questions are usually—at least while the peace is being kept—not bread-and-butter issues. Thus most people tend to paint their own foreign policy views with a very broad brush of generalizations.

This is not to suggest that specific answers cannot be given. Certainly, some very specific answers were given to question 3, which explores perceptions as to which is the most powerful in the world at present. Table 5.1 displays the response by nation. The results are suggestive of the European diversity alluded to above. None of the three countries shows a pattern of responses similar to any other. The British, by a landslide, see the United States behind the Soviet Union. Sixty-one out of one hundred Britons see the USSR as the world's most powerful nation. In Germany more credit is given to U.S. power, but half of the German population still sees the USSR as ahead. France is the country where U.S. power is still perceived as predominant. Fewer than one-third of the population sees the USSR as more powerful than the United States, while more than 55 percent of the French see the United States as ahead.

The sheer variety of views here underscores a point brought out earlier by Edward Luttwak to the effect that people in general—and a great many politicians—are not experts or even talented amateurs in gauging military potential. As a result, there is a good deal of room for manipulating perceptions. The difficulty with these three European allies is that all three of them cannot be right in their perceptions of the United States. At most, one of them is right. It may be that all three are wrong.

In the context of events preceding March 1980, the respondents may have underestimated the United States. Soviet armies were on the march while the United States was helpless to do anything about its hostages in Iran. Still to come was the rescue debacle in the desert. Some Europeans also had to

**TABLE 5.1: The Most Powerful Nation at Present (percent)**

| Most Powerful Nation | Britain | France | Germany |
|---|---|---|---|
| United States | 32 | 56 | 44 |
| USSR | 61 | 34 | 50 |
| Other nations | 7 | 10 | 6 |
| Total | 100 | 100 | 100 |
| N | 573 | 791 | 885 |

know that the U.S. military had not really enjoyed an unambiguous success in the field since the Inchon landings in the Korean war.

But responses to question 4, on the future of the military balance, suggested that if things are gloomy for U.S. power they are not unidirectionally optimistic for the USSR. The responses as to which nation is expected to be most powerful in 1985 (Table 5.2) suggest a European similarity of outlook that is not readily apparent, but of great importance once noticed. What is so striking about Table 5.2 is the fact that these respondents see the next five years as favoring not so much the United States or the Soviet Union, but some unknown third nation or bloc. The respondents were given a long list to choose from, including China, Japan, France, West Germany, the European Community, and the United Kingdom. The answers are widely scattered, but that should not obscure the main point: the perception of some kind of third power coming on the scene.

This may be one of those instances where the wish spawns the idea. There is a kind of pious hopefulness in this view, either for the emergence of a more congenial country as a third power or a neutralizing force constituted by the whole of Western Europe. Yet there is almost no reason to expect the supplanting of the two superpowers by a third country or group of countries. Even where the material capability exists—in Western Europe or Japan—there is no political will to arm to superpower level. Curiously, the respondents who say that a third power will appear in five years are probably the ones best equipped to know how implausible this response is. They are people who do not care to admit the trend toward Soviet dominance and its likely consequences, including the need to address European armament programs.

What the Europeans now think of U.S. power has strong implications for what they think of NATO. Even though it cannot be demonstrated statistically here, it is very likely that evaluations of NATO across time go hand in glove with perceptions of U.S. power. Tables 5.3 and 5.4 present responses to questions in which respondents were asked to compare the present balance between NATO and the Warsaw Pact (question 9), and the balance in five years (question 10).

**TABLE 5.2: The Most Powerful Nation in Five Years (percent)**

| Most Powerful Nation | Britain | France | Germany |
|---|---|---|---|
| United States | 27 | 39 | 36 |
| USSR | 59 | 31 | 44 |
| Other nations | 14 | 30 | 20 |
| Total | 100 | 100 | 100 |
| N | 789 | 594 | 834 |

## TABLE 5.3: Is NATO or the Warsaw Pact Stronger? (percent)

|  | Britain | France | Germany |
|---|---|---|---|
| NATO | 27 | 31 | 36 |
| Warsaw Pact | 50 | 31 | 44 |
| Equal | 11 | 0 | 20 |
| Don't know | 12 | 38 | 0 |
| Total | 100 | 100 | 100 |
| N | 967 | 993 | 1,001 |

## TABLE 5.4: The Comparative Strength of NATO and the Warsaw Pact in Five Years (percent)

|  | Britain | France | Germany |
|---|---|---|---|
| NATO | 25 | 22 | 33 |
| Warsaw Pact | 45 | 22 | 38 |
| Equal | 7 | 0 | 29 |
| Don't know | 23 | 56 | 0 |
| Total | 100 | 100 | 100 |
| N | 948 | 990 | 1,001 |

The coding categories are slightly different here from those used in Tables 5.1 and 5.2, but after sifting through the percentages, the same themes of diversity and uniformity appear. First, the only nation that sees NATO coming close in terms of power to the Warsaw Pact is France. The British are, again, the most pessimistic, followed by the Germans. Looking down the road five years, there is no change seen in the NATO/Warsaw Pact balance; instead, there is just an increase in uncertainty.

### THE PATH TO EUROPEAN SECURITY

If one assimilates these four questions dealing with perceptions of the present and future balance between the East and the West, there is evidence to suggest that public opinion in the three most powerful European nations has come to accept the notion of Western inferiority in terms of military power. The difficulty from this point on is trying to find out what kinds of conclusions can be drawn from this outlook.

A logical way to approach this line of inquiry is to take up the question of security arrangements, the subject of question 5, which suggested several possibilities including NATO, a European defense command with ties to the United States, a similar defense command not allied to the United States, a strictly national force, and finally accommodation of the Soviet Union. Essentially, the first two choices involved continuation of the Atlantic orientation of European defenses, while the others represented increasingly isolationist and accommodationist approaches. The material in Table 5.5 shows how the choices are distributed by nation. This is an object lesson in how national publics can draw a variety of inferences that seem hardly connected, at first, to a diversity of premises. Take, for example, the British. No nation of the three has less confidence in U.S. power, nor more respect for the Warsaw Pact—either presently or five years hence. One could be forgiven for hypothesizing that this kind of pessimism would make the British the leading appeasers of Europe. At a minimum, they should have scant faith in NATO. The French, on the contrary, should have a good deal of faith in NATO, or at least in an Atlantic alliance structure, given their relative faith in U.S. power. As for the Germans, they should be somewhere in the middle.

Instead, what one finds is that nearly 90 percent of the Germans see NATO or a Euro-American alliance as the best security structure. The British, as pessimistic as they are about Western power, follow the Germans (about 70 percent favoring NATO or a Euro-American structure). The really great difference is found with the French. While the single largest group (33 percent) prefers a Euro-American alliance, the French show markedly more interest in European neutralism (24 percent), French isolationism (22 percent), and appeasement (8 percent) than citizens of the other two major European powers. Perhaps this attitudinal range could be explained by their relatively low estimation of Soviet power. Essentially, however, the kind of logic being applied here states that confidence in U.S. power erodes support for NATO and a Euro-American alliance, while fear of the Soviet Union tends to enhance support. In the case of the French, it might also bear pointing out that a certain kind of strategic Gaullism seems to have been internalized by the public. It might be added that no nation of the three is more internally divided among strategic choices than France.

**TABLE 5.5: What Is the Best Way to Provide Security? (percent)**

|  | Britain | France | Germany |
|---|---|---|---|
| NATO | 50 | 13 | 58 |
| Europe and the U.S. | 21 | 33 | 30 |
| Europe alone | 10 | 24 | 6 |
| National force | 14 | 22 | 4 |
| Appease USSR | 5 | 8 | 2 |
| Total | 100 | 100 | 100 |
| N | 853 | 766 | 851 |

In order to provide analytic depth to the Europeans' choices of alliance structures, an attempt was made to link their choices to their perceptions of power. Table 5.5 simply looked at the choices country by country. Tables 5.6, 5.7, and 5.8 offer more insights since, on a country-by-country basis, they show how perceptions of relative superpower strength affect choices of security arrangements. There are some odd findings in these tables. Turning to Britain, for example, it is striking that while the country shows a high overall support for an Atlantic security structure and, simultaneously, a relatively low regard for U.S. power vis-à-vis that of the USSR, views of East-West power balances have remarkably little effect on the choices of the best security arrangement. Though the authors are very cautious when it comes to using tests of statistical significance when the issue happens to be of political significance, it is only fair to pass on that the chi-square test for this table does not attain a modest 0.05 level of significance (that is, the percentage differences among the various cells may well be just a function of sampling error). In effect, perceptions of U.S. power may affect Britain as a whole but not really serve to differentiate perceptions among individual Britons. This is even more obvious in the case of the Germans. They show very little difference in opinion about alliance structure across various categories of power perception (Table 5.7). The French, again, form an exceptional group. Not only does the country show idiosyncratic characteristics as a nation, but so do French citizens as individual respondents. Table 5.8 tells a good deal about French thinking on the connection between power and structure. Those who see the Americans as most powerful (the bulk of the French) have very scant approval of either NATO (12 percent) or appeasement (6 percent). Those who see the USSR as more powerful are more in favor of either NATO (14 percent) or appeasement (13 percent). The basic rule, then, is that in France perceptions of U.S. preponderance tend to cluster the French into independent and isolationist positions; perceptions of Soviet preponderance tend to drive French respondents into the diametrically opposed solutions of NATO or accommodation to Soviet positions. With Britain and Germany, on the other hand, there is an individual-level independence of power perception and security preference.

Does any of this make any sense? It is possible to take each country on a kind of ad-hoc basis and find excuses for its behavior: the French are only being logical, while the depressed Britons and the nuclearly toothless Germans have no choice but to depend on the United States. But these kinds of gross generalizations, while appealing to the intuitions of some, are not very satisfactory theoretically. What is being dealt with here is a situation in which certain stimuli, perceptions of U.S. and Western power, lead to different responses among the major countries of Western Europe. Nationality, just by itself, can play an important intervening role; however, there may be other kinds of predispositions more significant than nationality that play a role here and require identification.

### TABLE 5.6: Maximum Security and Perceptions of National Power: Great Britain (percent)

| | Greatest National Power | |
|---|---|---|
| Security Structure | U.S. | USSR |
| NATO | 49 | 53 |
| Europe and the U.S. | 25 | 22 |
| Europe alone | 10 | 8 |
| National force | 12 | 13 |
| Appease USSR | 4 | 4 |
| N | 260 | 454 |

Note: 1 out of 15 (6.7%) of the valid cells have expected cell frequency less than 5.

### TABLE 5.7: Maximum Security and Perceptions of National Power: Germany

| | Greatest National Power | |
|---|---|---|
| Security Structure | U.S. | USSR |
| NATO | 57 | 60 |
| Europe and the U.S. | 33 | 28 |
| Europe alone | 7 | 6 |
| National force | 1 | 4 |
| Appease USSR | 2 | 2 |
| N | 349 | 395 |

Note: 3 out of 15 (20%) of the valid cells have expected cell frequency less than 5.

### TABLE 5.8: Maximum Security and Perceptions of National Power: France

| | Greatest National Power | |
|---|---|---|
| Security Structure | U.S. | USSR |
| NATO | 12 | 14 |
| Europe and the U.S. | 37 | 35 |
| Europe alone | 25 | 20 |
| National force | 20 | 18 |
| Appease USSR | 6 | 12 |
| N | 368 | 231 |

Note: 1 out of 15 (6.8%) of the valid cells have expected cell frequency less than 5.

At this juncture, it is useful to take an inventory of this study's findings that will assist in understanding some of the following material:

- There are wide variations in perceptions of U.S. and NATO strength in America's greatest allies in Europe.
- Especially the British, but also the Germans, are very pessimistic about the U.S. and Western position relative to that of the Soviet Union. At the least, they see the West as weaker, and becoming more so.
- The French are, in contrast, more confident about Western power compared to that of the USSR.
- Despite their misgivings about Western power, the British and Germans still see NATO and/or a Euro-American alliance as the preferred way to provide for security.
- The French are markedly more in favor of exclusively European or national-level security arrangements. NATO is not popular; isolationism is.
- In Britain and Germany, an individual's perceptions of the East-West power balance does not directly affect his or her attitude toward security arrangements and alliance structure.
- In France, favorable perceptions of U.S. and NATO power are associated with preferences for independent European or national-level security postures. Those more impressed by Soviet power prefer either more intimate relations with NATO or further accommodation with the Soviet Union.

If there is an underlying theme here, it is that neither bellicosity nor saber rattling are univocal in effect. There are complicated mechanisms connecting military power, its perceptions, and public opinion. At the most general level, nationality can be used to explain variance. But what one really wants to know is whether or not one can explain signs of neutralist, perhaps even Finlandized, opinion in Europe in terms of what either the Americans or Soviets are doing. This, in turn, is likely to be affected by what role Europeans would like to see any alliances play in the world and by Europeans' willingness to make a significant effort to defend themselves.

## THE EUROPEAN COMMITMENT TO DEFENSE

How willing are Europeans to make a defense effort? What it is that constitutes a defense effort, in the first place, is controversial. United States authorities like to measure defense effort in terms of proportion of GNP per capita to the military establishment. This makes the United States compare favorably with its allies, and yet it looks peace loving compared to the Soviets. The U.S. figure for 1978 was slightly above 5 percent, those for Great Britain, France, and Germany between 5 and 3.5 percent, and for the Soviet Union more than 10 percent.[3] The trends for the four NATO allies can be seen in Figure 5.1.

Europeans argue, with a good deal of credibility, that they make a greater effort in manpower since, in most continental NATO member states, one form of conscription or another is practiced. As militant as the mood may be in the United States regarding defense, the consensus on the defense effort is in weapons acquisition expenditures, not yet in initiating a new draft. Still, willingness to spend on defense is a useful indicator of how individuals think about defense. In question 7, those interviewed were asked if they felt the level of their country's expenditures for military purposes should be increased, decreased, or left at the present level. Table 5.9 shows the assorted responses for the countries under examination here. This table, as much as anything seen so far, is suggestive of what commentators have in mind when they discuss neutralism or Finlandization in Europe. But the table itself does not *prove* Finlandization. Arguing for alterations in the defense budget, whether one discusses increases or decreases, must be seen within the contemporary security context. The authors have already outlined their views on what that context is and how dangerous it appears to be, although there is, of course, room for debate. Still, is the military situation in Western Europe so unclear that a

**FIGURE 5.1: Percentage of GNP Spent on Military, 1969 to 1978**

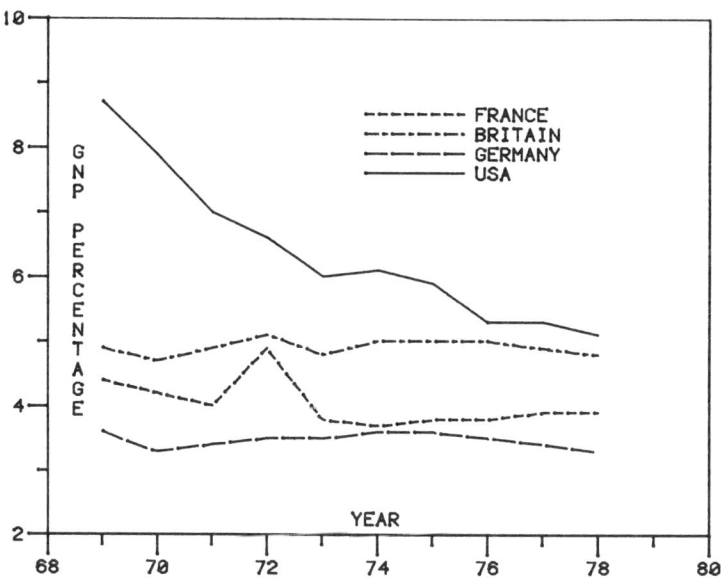

Source: U.S. Arms Control and Disarmament Agency, World Military Expenditures and Arms Transfers, 1969-1978 (Washington, D.C., 1980).

**TABLE 5.9: The Level of Military Expenditures (percent)**

|               | Britain | France | Germany |
|---------------|---------|--------|---------|
| Increased     | 54      | 17     | 24      |
| Left the same | 10      | 58     | 61      |
| Decreased     | 36      | 25     | 15      |
| Total         | 100     | 100    | 100     |
| N             | 903     | 865    | 844     |

majority of Britons (54 percent) sees a need for increased defense expenditures, while a majority of French (58 percent) and Germans (61 percent) feels expenditures are adequate? Yet, in spite of the British majority for increased defense expenditures, a substantial majority of respondents in the United Kingdom want these expenditures cut, and one out of four French citizens feels the same way. The Germans seemed to be the least eager to follow this option. What is suggested here is that the major allies (except for Britain and the United States) are not quite on the same wavelength. Of course, even the United States and Britain may be drifting apart in the proximate future.

From 1980 to 1981, the public's support for defense spending decreased in much of Western Europe. While support for increased defense spending remained highest in Britain compared to other European NATO countries, it dropped 28 percent in April 1981, with 47 percent opting to keep it on the same level.[4]

On May 28, 1981, President Mitterand's foreign minister, Claude Cheysson, was asked during an interview with reporters from *Le Monde* if there were a danger of neutralism in Europe. He replied:

> This is a latent danger. I know Britain well and I often refer to it. In my view, it is one of the world's greatest countries. But that a neutralist trend, in the strict sense of the term, can develop in Britain amazes me.
>
> In other places, it is understandable. But in an old country like that, it is amazing. So I tell you: Yes, there is a danger of neutralism. It results from a desire to give up, from a great weariness, and it causes me to despair. I see far less of this danger in France. It is a rather remarkable sign of health.[5]

The situation is even more pronounced in Italy, the Netherlands, and Belgium, where only one in ten or fewer wanted an increased defense budget by the end of 1980; 39 percent in Italy, 34 percent in Belgium, and 31 percent in the Netherlands opted for decreased defense spending. The remainder in these three countries favored retaining the current level of expenditures.[6]

The lack of substantial support for increased defense spending in Germany is a manifestation of a strong pacifist and neutralist attitude among many

Germans, especially the youth. It parallels increasingly large demonstrations in several German cities in the spring and summer of 1981 protesting the planned deployment of U.S. medium-range nuclear weapons in Western Europe and particularly in Germany. It also reflects apprehension about the declining economic situation in the Federal Republic of Germany[7] and the continuing, largely emotional, concern that growing confrontations between East and West might adversely affect any future cooperation and rapprochement between the two halves of divided Germany.

There is a further point on the issue of European commitment to defense that needs to be inserted here. "How much?" for defense is clearly an important question; but so is "defense of what?" Question number 6 explored the respondent's view whether NATO should just provide security against a possible Soviet attack in Western Europe, or whether it should also help protect the NATO members' vital interests in other parts of the world.

The motive behind this question is fairly obvious from a U.S. point of view: it was posed at a time when the U.S. administration was mulling over a major new commitment to the defense of a critical strategic zone made all the more critical by Iranian radicalism and Soviet intervention in Afghanistan. The United States wanted to know then how Europeans felt about expanding the scope of NATO beyond the limits of the Tropic of Cancer. Any specific arrangements for establishing the design of the Persian Gulf's defense appear to be far away. But the United States may have to make some of those arrangements at the apparent expense of NATO. The word "apparent" is used only because one cannot think of defending one's flanks as equivalent to a policy of abandoning one's center.

In Table 5.10 there is a suggestion that the British and French publics understand that NATO has an implicit global role that may have to become explicit. In any event, there is support for extending NATO's reach in those countries. Germany, however, appears to show some symptoms of an inclination toward Euroisolationism. One should not make too much of these differences. After all, it is still the case that an appreciable majority (57 percent) of Germans expressing an opinion sees a need to expand NATO's geographic horizons. Nevertheless, they lag well behind the British and the French in this respect.

**TABLE 5.10: The Geographic Limits for NATO (percent)**

|                | Britain | France | Germany |
|----------------|---------|--------|---------|
| Western Europe | 24      | 30     | 43      |
| Elsewhere      | 76      | 70     | 57      |
| Total          | 100     | 100    | 100     |
| N              | 845     | 660    | 835     |

## A TREND TOWARD FINLANDIZATION?

If one steps back for a few moments and dwells on the material in Tables 5.9 and 5.10, one is forced to confront the fact that within these three countries there is no consensus on defense spending and an appreciable divergence of views on NATO's defense role. If one adds to this what is known from daily headlines about Western European squeamishness about long-range theater nuclear force (LRTNF) deployments by the United States, even in the face of accelerated Soviet deployment, it is not difficult to argue that a process of Finlandization has set in, even though it is far from a completed process.* What, however, explains it?

Answering this question with the assistance of survey research data requires one to develop an "operationalized measure" of Finlandization. This will be done by focusing on tendencies toward Finlandization by combining information from responses to two questions already discussed—question 5 on preferred security structure (Tables 5.5 and 5.6) and question 7 on defense expenditures (Table 5.9).

The assumptions behind this operationalization are that from a Soviet point of view it would be highly desirable if European governments were to pry the United States military out of their national territories by developing a European-only alliance, separate national defense structures, or by adopting a policy of accommodation to Soviet wishes. Furthermore, it would be greatly in the Soviet interest to see Europeans freeze or reduce defense spending. From this perspective, the "ideal European" would be one who wants to accommodate the USSR and cut defense spending. Fortunately, this kind of European is fairly rare. Yet there are Europeans who want to cut arms spending just as there are Europeans who object to the U.S. military presence on the Continent. There are some who want both—no Americans and no arms spending. Then there are those who prefer either NATO or a Euro-American alliance and increased arms spending. These people will be called "Eurohawks"—with full knowledge that it is a kind of exaggerated shorthand term. By implication, those who are not Eurohawks are "Eurodoves." With more questions available, a more refined measure could have been developed. But the Eurohawk-Eurodove dichotomy does provide great economy in expression.

The Eurohawk-Eurodove variable is being used primarily for one purpose: to try to shed some light on what might explain trends toward Finlandization in public opinion. (One suspects that European elites are much more Finlandized than the masses.) Eurodoves are distributed in Britain, France, and Germany

---

*Finlandization is the adoption by a European country of a foreign policy like that of Finland, which seeks to maintain friendly relations with the Soviet Union, usually by acceding to pressure from the Soviet government. (*World Book Dictionary*, Chicago World Book-Childcraft International, 1980.)

in differing proportions. In Britain, slightly more than half (54 percent) fall into the dovish category; in France, the proportion is even greater (82 percent); and in Germany, 65 percent of the population can be classified as Eurodoves. These are both politically and statistically significant differences. Indeed, the political differences overshadow the statistical differences. For example, the high rate of Eurodovism in France is a phenomenon that is quite distinct from Eurodovism in Germany or Britain. French foreign policy has been openly interventionist in certain parts of the world; its weapons acquisition policy is one of continuing nuclearization at both the strategic and battlefield levels. What makes the French appear so Eurodovish is their internalization at the level of public opinion of the Gaullist notion that France can be part of the Atlantic alliance without being in NATO.

The authors think they are on the right track in approaching the Eurodove-Eurohawk dichotomy from two aspects: alignment with NATO and willingness to shoulder increased arms costs. But the measure employed here has to be interpreted with some sensitivity. From the point of view of calibration, it probably exaggerates French Eurodovism. Furthermore, the authors do not want to suggest that questioning either NATO or increased arms expenditures points to individual Finlandization. Finlandization is a collective policy of military isolation from the United States combined with insufficient domestic military resources to guarantee independence from the Soviet Union.

This raises the question of the relationship between Eurodovism and perceptions of Soviet power. Have Soviet authorities been able to buy Finlandization (or at least make a down payment on it) with their arms buildup? It has been an impressive buildup. But the authors suspect that part of the European reaction has been affected by the United States. Speaking of the dangers of Soviet military growth, a 1981 USICA document quotes Raymond Aaron's assessment of the pattern of thinking in Europe: "They recognize the danger but they are pretending to disregard it because they are doubtful of the present strength of the United States."[8]

## THE FACTOR OF U.S. RESOLVE

Eurodovism, however, is not solely a function of perceptions of power alone. As seen earlier, perceptions of power produce indeterminate effects on opinion. In terms of estimating the actual arms balance, the European publics are not far off the mark in a limited sense. Even though the countries differ in their exact estimates, they all still view the United States as at least competitive with the USSR in superpower terms. It cannot be just material balances alone that are affecting European opinion. In fact, estimates of relative military strength have a very modest, almost surprising, impact on how Europeans view security arrangements.

Take, for example, the case of the Germans. Keep in mind that the German population is about evenly split in its estimate of which superpower is ahead. But when queried about the best way to provide security, it made little difference what one thought of the Americans or the Soviets. No matter which side individuals saw ahead, almost 60 percent favored NATO for protection. Soviet arms, alone, are not Finlandizing Germany. Likewise, perceptions of power do not significantly affect opinions in Germany on arms expenditure decisions. Of those who see the United States ahead, 12 percent want to cut spending; among those who see the Soviets ahead, the proportion grows only to 16 percent.

Turning to Britain and France, the same general rule of very weak relationships between strength perception and policy consequences (alliance structure and arms procurement) holds. But when the question of power is raised in a slightly different way, things clear up considerably. Question 8 was the most revealing of the questions asked in the survey, delving into the degree of confidence the respondent had in the United States to come to Western Europe's defense. Table 5.11 shows the country-by-country distribution of replies.

Within each nation there is evidence of very healthy associations between perceptions of resolve and conclusions individuals reach about alliance structure and arms budgets. Taking the Germans as a case in point, almost three-quarters of those who have a "great deal" of confidence in the United States prefer NATO as the best guarantee of security (74 percent). Correspondingly, less than a third (31 percent) of those with no confidence at all in the United States prefer NATO. Similar patterns hold for the British and French. The basic rule is that it is less the power of the United States and more its resolve to use what power it has that affects European commitment to NATO and to their own defense efforts. The more Europeans have confidence that the United States will intervene to help them, the more appropriate NATO seems to be, and the more support for arms expenditures. Essentially, many Eurodoves are not showing signs of liking for the Soviet Union or even distaste for the United States. Instead, it is just a lack of confidence in American "will" to aid Europe.

**TABLE 5.11: Confidence in U.S. Resolve to Defend Europe (percent)**

|  | Britain | France | Germany |
|---|---|---|---|
| Great deal | 34 | 21 | 18 |
| Fair amount | 40 | 52 | 55 |
| Not much | 18 | 21 | 23 |
| None at all | 8 | 6 | 4 |
| Total | 100 | 100 | 100 |
| N | 940 | 869 | 907 |

The relationship between an estimate of the U.S. military position vis-à-vis that of the USSR, confidence in the United States, and Eurodovism can be visualized in Figure 5.2. Remember that classification as a Eurodove has been accomplished by taking into account how respondents evaluated the alliance with the United States and the idea of increased arms spending.

Within the figure there are two lines, one solid, one dashed, for each country under consideration. The higher the line the greater the proportion of Eurodoves in the sample. The solid lines represent those respondents who see the United States as a superior military power; the dashed lines represent those who see the Soviet Union as superior militarily. The left-hand ends of the lines illustrate the proportions of Eurodoves among those who are confident of the U.S. commitment to defend Western Europe. The right-hand ends of the lines show the proportions of Eurodoves among those who doubt that basic commitment.

The basic question that led to the construction of the figure was simply this: how do perceptions of power and perceptions of resolve affect pacifist or neutralist tendencies?

The overall impression is clearly one of greater changes in opinions being a function of evaluations of U.S. will rather than U.S. arms. This is hardly

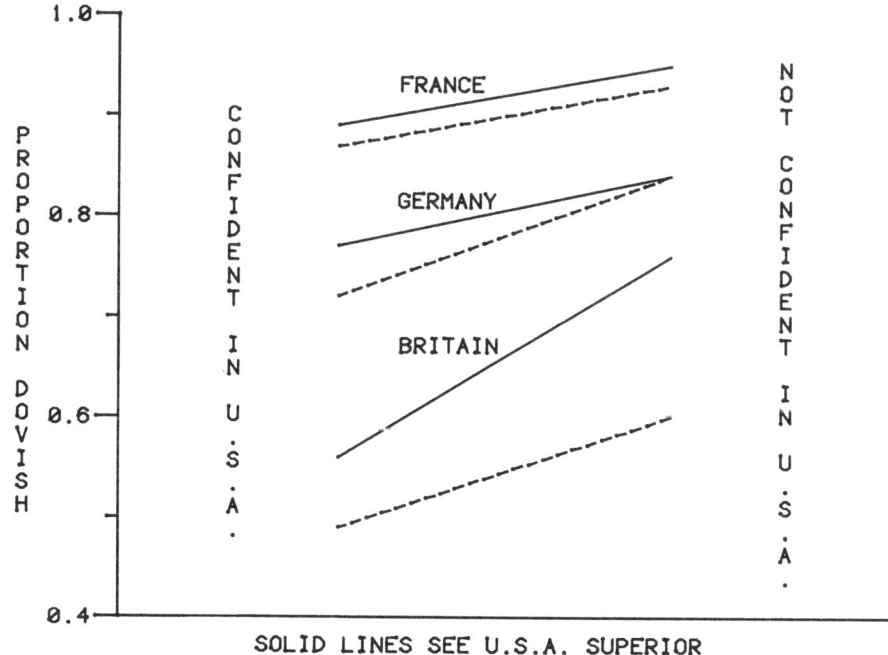

**FIGURE 5.2: Power, Confidence, and the Eurodoves**

SOLID LINES SEE U.S.A. SUPERIOR
DASHED LINES SEE U.S.S.R. SUPERIOR

counterintuitive. It makes a good deal of sense, in fact. However, the authors did not expect this clearly "political" judgment to statistically overwhelm "material" factors. If everything in a material sense were equal, then, of course, political factors would be paramount. But the material factors as represented by the military balance are at present no better than one of "essential equivalence," obviously a rather nebulous term. What one seems to be able to argue, no matter how imprecise measurement may be, is that no U.S. administration can elicit full confidence in its resolve from Europeans with armaments programs by themselves. This is a complicating factor, since demonstrations of resolve, outside of just bigger budgets, are hard to be conjured in the eyes of some Europeans. The Carter-initiated grain embargo is a good case in point. While it was intended to show resolve by punishing the Soviet Union for the Afghanistan invasion, to the extent the American action was painful to the American people, it is doubtful that it accomplished its intended purpose. Of course, it is not clear either what Reagan hoped to accomplish by lifting the embargo.

In more general terms, it appears that European public opinion regarding NATO and the entire notion of alliance with the United States (and resistance to the aims of the Soviet Union) is responding in a pattern that is very Clausewitzian. In the opening chapter of *On War*, Clausewitz pointed out:

> When whole communities go to war—whole peoples, and especially *civilized* peoples—the reason always lies in some political situation, and the occasion is always due to some political object.[9]

A paragraph later he added: "The political object is the goal, war is the means of reaching it, and means can never be considered in isolation from their purpose."[10]

From this perspective, the Europeans' way of dividing themselves into hawks and doves more along lines of perception of will than perception of means makes perfect sense. But conveying will is harder than projecting means, at least for the United States. Its weapons systems—those currently operational and those planned to be acquired—are directed toward winning battles. Winning battles is what military tactics are all about. It is strategy, by contrast, that provides a basis for getting into or avoiding a battle in the first place. Strategy provides a motive for the exercise of will. But the rules of strategy are theoretical and long term; strategy calls for skills and habits of mind that clash with Luttwak's apt characterization of Americans as "problem-solvers rather than systematic or long-range thinkers." But if the European public's support of U.S. policy in Europe depends greatly upon perception of American will, then Luttwak is completely correct in asserting that "to achieve even moderate success the nation's external policy must be guided by the alien rules of strategy."[11] What the United States does best—

the engineering of lethality—is not directly addressable to the major problem, which is conveying an understanding of lethality for what?

That is a purely political question rather than a military one. The data are quite unambiguous (for survey research data) on just how intensely political—to the exclusion of almost any other variable—orientations toward the Euro-American alliance and shoring up its means are.

## THE INFLUENCE OF PARTY AFFILIATION

It is already known that Eurodoves and Eurohawks are distinguishable by their confidence in the United States. While one cannot incontestably prove it, it is probably the confidence, or the lack of it, that creates hawks or doves—rather than the other way around. What else can be used to tell who falls into the categories of Eurodoves and Eurohawks? To put things very broadly, it is largely a matter of a hawkish European right and a dovish European left. That should surprise no one by itself. Indeed, in the United States as well, the right tends to be more hawkish and the left more dovish. However, in Europe the situation is more complicated, at least from the U.S. perspective, since the appearance that the Italian Communist Party gives of being sympathetic of Italy's membership in NATO clashes with the appearance that the British Labour Party wants to pull Britain out of NATO. This is counterintuitive, yet not really any more so than the refusal of Republicans and Democrats to fit into ideological molds that Europeans can refer to.

If one turns to a left-right instance (see Table 5.12)—Britain is convenient here because of the relative simplicity of its party system as of March 1980—it is readily apparent that there is a fairly consistent progression from hawkishness to dovishness as one moves from the Conservatives to the Liberals and on to Labour. The actual strength of the association (Cramer's V = 0.217) is moderately high. To a large extent, one expects Conservatives and Labourites to disagree on many issues. The conventional view of British politics held by almost unanimously admiring American political scientists has been one of a laudably crisp differentiation between Britain's two major parties—a differentiation that has been sometimes longed for by political scientists in the U.S.

**TABLE 5.12: The Impact of Party Affiliation in Britain (percent)**

|  | Conservative | Liberal | Labour |
|---|---|---|---|
| Hawk | 55 | 37 | 32 |
| Dove | 45 | 63 | 68 |
| Total | 100 | 100 | 100 |
| N | 292 | 93 | 292 |

party system. But underlying the differences between the two parties, it was felt, were organic links that held the country together. The situation has changed a bit in the 1980s: "What does seem clear is that the traditional bonds of social class, party, and common nationality are waning, and with them the old restraints of hierarchy and deference."[12]

One is not sure that the fact that nearly two out of three identifiers with the Labour Party show signs of isolationism and suspicion of more military spending can be explained, usefully, in terms of a decline of British political culture; nor should one be convinced, as Cheysson says he is (as cited earlier), that this phenomenon is due to British weariness. But these are very plausible arguments, and the value of Cheysson's views are not weakened by the observation that they are a bit self-serving. French politicians can do themselves no harm by delivering a sidelong insult to British combativeness. Furthermore, it is very much in the French national interest that Britain remain tied close enough to NATO to insure the deployment of the U.S. ground-launched cruise missile, even if the British have to be shamed into it.

## THE INFLUENCE OF OTHER SOCIOECONOMIC INDICATORS

While partisanship clearly does affect the respondents' answers bearing on the dove-hawk dichotomy, what is the influence of the conventional socioeconomic indicators that have been correlated with support for either Labour or Conservative voting in Britain? In other words, how is not only partisanship but the basis of partisanship connected to foreign policy opinions in what is supposed to be a class-conscious society? Table 5.13, which displays the relationship between occupation and foreign policy orientation, indicates that the percentage differences that show up are not suggestive of the kind of linear or monotonic pattern normally expected. Moreover, the table falls short of the minimum critical value for the chi-square statistic acceptable for significance. But even with a larger sample that might confirm the patterns in this table, one might be hard pressed to explain what the table really tells us

**TABLE 5.13: The Impact of Occupation (percent)**

|       | Unskilled | Semi-skilled | Skilled | Clerical, Sales | Professional, Management, Administrative |
|-------|-----------|--------------|---------|-----------------|------------------------------------------|
| Hawk  | 34        | 39           | 45      | 44              | 45                                       |
| Dove  | 66        | 61           | 55      | 56              | 55                                       |
| Total | 100       | 100          | 100     | 100             | 100                                      |
| N     | 133       | 102          | 161     | 198             | 151                                      |

other than that occupation has no clear relationship to dovishness or hawkishness, except that the unskilled and semiskilled are clearly more dovish than the rest of the labor force.

This brings us to education as a possible influential factor for the dove-hawk dichotomy. It should be noted here that upper educational levels in Britain cannot be equated with upper class or high status, although accent (George Bernard Shaw's litmus test for class) is losing the certain reliability it once had as a status indicator. Part of this is due to increased educational and cultural opportunities, not the least of which is television. But the British educational system is still far from egalitarian in terms of recruitment or the kinds of graduates it turns out. Still, as Table 5.14 shows, there is no appreciable difference in terms of the foreign policy outlook under discussion here across the entire spectrum of British educational attainment. This must be one of the few instances in which education simply has a random impact on an important foreign policy position. Of course, random is meant here only in a probabilistic sense. With a more extensive questionnaire, one might well find relevant differences in the responses.

It might be objected that occupation and education are not, by themselves, appropriate ways to classify Britons. The authors certainly agree that the concept of "class," in the way it has played a role in Britain, is as much a psychological or social-psychological matter as it might be socioeconomic. Hence, if one allows the respondents to categorize themselves into the working class or the nonworking class, as the questionnaire for Britain permits, one might obtain a more accurate reading. Table 5.15, which shows the impact of subjective social class on the distribution of hawkishness and dovishness, indicates that the objective measures have not been misleading. Again, the relationship is just plain negligible. However, when class membership—either objective or psychological—leads to something as explicit as joining a trade union (that is, when one turns from classification to behavior), significant relationships begin to appear. In Table 5.16, the 12 percent difference between members and nonmembers of unions is appreciable. Perhaps "appreciable" is a bit of a weasel word. As an alternative, one can report that the value of Cramer's V of Phi = 0.11 is a little bit more than half as strong as the rela-

**TABLE 5.14: The Impact of Education Based on Age that Schooling Was Completed (percent)**

|       | 14  | 15  | 16-18 | 19  |
|-------|-----|-----|-------|-----|
| Hawk  | 40  | 39  | 47    | 44  |
| Dove  | 60  | 61  | 53    | 66  |
| Total | 100 | 100 | 100   | 100 |
| N     | 204 | 188 | 287   | 126 |

**TABLE 5.15: The Impact of Social Class by Self-Categorization (percent)**

|  | Nonworking | Working |
|---|---|---|
| Hawk | 43 | 39 |
| Dove | 57 | 61 |
| Total | 100 | 100 |
| N | 422 | 348 |

tionship found to exist for party affiliation. This is perfectly in accord with what one would expect, given the strong formal overlap between union membership and Labour Party membership that exists in Britain.

At this juncture, one should reiterate the importance of noting that partisanship, almost exclusively, correlated with the dichotomy between doves and hawks which, in turn, was based on British inclinations toward neutralism or strong support of NATO defense. There is something about partisanship, by itself, that contributes to British evaluations of their basic strategic options. But in this evaluation of options, perceptions of the United States' will to defend Europe play a strikingly clear role. Table 5.17 summarizes several separately computed tables that illustrate just what the role of perceptions is.

The tale told in the table is one of how perceptions aggravate differences between and within the parties. Going across the rows, one sees in most instances the familiar progression of increasing neutralist responses from the political right to the political left. But, as one goes down each column, the percentages also tend to increase. That is, within each party increasingly unfavorable perceptions of U.S. resolve add to neutralist tendencies. The situation is much more dramatic for the Conservatives. The Conservatives with a "great deal" of confidence in the United States show only slightly more than a one in three rate of Eurodovism. The small number with no confidence at all in the United States have a three out of four rate of Eurodovism. In the Labour Party the differences for the "great deal"–"none at all" pair of categories is much less: 60 to 79 percent. But in either major party and in the case of the Liberals as well, there are important intraparty differences brought about by perceptions of U.S. resolve.

There is probably little any U.S. administration can do about the underlying suspicion in the Labour Party of military expenditures or NATO. The dislike of military expenditures is, in fact, not really a Labour Party monopoly. On the other hand, the dislike of NATO is now at a point where the Labourites have actually split into an avowedly neutralist and isolationist (such as, in terms of withdrawal from the EEC) bloc and a more internationalist social democratic bloc. The former group is, from what is known of them beyond being influenced by American behavior or assurances. But the social democratic element in

### TABLE 5.16: The Impact of Union Membership (percent)

|  | Members | Nonmembers |
|---|---|---|
| Hawk | 34 | 46 |
| Dove | 66 | 54 |
| Total | 100 | 100 |
| N | 303 | 507 |

### TABLE 5.17: Partisanship and Neutralism in Britain: How Perceptions of U.S. Commitment Play a Role (percent)

| Confidence in United States | Conservative | Liberal | Labour | Overall |
|---|---|---|---|---|
| Great deal | 36 | 47 | 60 | 47 |
|  | (108) | (30) | (91) | (229) |
| Fair amount | 46 | 56 | 60 | 53 |
|  | (118) | (32) | (112) | (262) |
| Not much | 43 | 57 | 70 | 57 |
|  | (49) | (19) | (52) | (120) |
| None at all | 77 | 80 | 79 | 78 |
|  | (13) | (10) | (28) | (51) |

Note: Percentages refer to proportion in each cell giving a neutralist or dovish response. Numbers in parentheses are bases for percentages.

Britain, at least a minority of them, may well be the kinds of Britons who will evaluate their nation's strategic posture and involvement in Europe with an eye to what the United States ends up doing.

### PARTY INFLUENCES ON THE CONTINENT

If one starts to put some of the pieces together of what is known about the impact of the perception of U.S. will, the relative unimportance of personal background characteristics,[13] and the structuring role played by right-left orientation, one can ask whether or not party influence on the Continent is similar to that in Britain. This is not an easy question to answer for several reasons. One is purely technical: in the surveys provided and employed here, there is no partisan information available from Germany; on the other hand, there is such information available on France.

Before assessing the influence of party affiliation in France, one should compare Britain, France, and Germany in terms of how perceptions of the United States affect the incidence of neutralist tendencies. Such a comparison is suggestive of both national differences peculiar to each country and of certain international uniformities. Table 5.18 summarizes much of what is already known about the kind of shape in which the Western alliance finds itself and even explains part of the problem, at least the part attributable to the United States. Indeed, no matter how one looks at these data, no matter how many statistical controls one applies, nothing seems to alter the crucial role played by perceptions of the United States. Dovishness increases as confidence in the United States decreases; France and Germany show great changes in strategic outlook for any change in level of confidence in the United States.

The case of the French is particularly troubling since, as can be seen from Table 5.19, they appear to be more dovish than impressionistic evidence would suggest. That is, the very high levels of dovishness clash with President Mitterand's defense procurement decisions to date, specifically his decision to add more missile-carrying submarines to the French fleet. The reason the French appear as dovish as they do is largely caused by the conjoint effects of the French Communist Party's opposition to weapons they know to be directed at the Soviet Union and to the lingering impact of Gaullism—an impact that keeps French public opinion suspicious of force integration with NATO. Even though it is hard to find two parties more dissimilar in either philosophy or organizational style, they have both pursued policies on occasion that coincide with the interests of the Soviet Union.

In the case of Germany, there is nothing that can be said directly about partisan differences with the evidence available. However, one can draw some

**TABLE 5.18: Confidence in the United States and Neutralist Tendencies: Evidence from Three Allies (percent)**

| Confidence in the United States | Britain Gamma 0.17 | France Gamma 0.32 | Germany Gamma 0.32 |
|---|---|---|---|
| Great deal | 55 | 84 | 61 |
|  | (277) | (151) | (137) |
| Fair amount | 55 | 91 | 79 |
|  | (309) | (356) | (411) |
| Not much | 63 | 94 | 83 |
|  | (145) | (132) | (171) |
| None at all | 81 | 94 | 86 |
|  | (62) | (36) | (28) |
| Overall | 58 | 90 | 77 |
|  | (793) | (675) | (747) |

*Note:* Percentages refer to proportion in each cell giving a neutralist or dovish response. Numbers in parentheses are bases for percentages.

### TABLE 5.19: Major French Political Parties and Strategic Outlook, 1980 (percent)

| Outlook | Party Affiliation | | | |
|---|---|---|---|---|
| | PCF[a] | PS[b] | UDF[c] | RPR[d] |
| Hawk | 0 | 6 | 14 | 27 |
| Dove | 100 | 94 | 86 | 73 |
| Total | 100 | 100 | 100 | 100 |
| N | 78 | 238 | 170 | 67 |

[a] French Communist Party
[b] Socialist Party
[c] French Democratic Union
[d] Rally for the Republic (Gaullists)

inferences from secondary data presented in Table 5.20, which offers a party breakdown of the replies to questions about the preferred security arrangements that were analyzed in Tables 5.5 to 5.8. Clearly, support for NATO is lowest in the ranks of the Social Democrats (SPD) (43 percent) compared to 58 and 57 percent among the adherents of the Christian Democratic Union/ Christian Social Union (CDU/CSU) and the Free Democrats Union (FDP). Moreover, the SDP adherents opt to a much higher degree for either an independent West European defense force allied with the United States (24 percent) or independent (12 percent) than followers of the other two parties; they are also the strongest supporters for accommodating the Soviet Union, although the percentage is only 4 percent. This confirms what is already well known: the most outspoken German Eurodoves come from the SPD, and most likely from its left wing. What is more important, perhaps, is the fact that even without regard to partisanship, Germany shows the greatest neutralist tendency of the larger NATO partners. The background data that are available on German respondents—education, occupation, and (uniquely for Germany) religion—suggest that opposition to military spending and suspicion of alliance with the United States is evenly spread throughout German society. Germany is quite like Britain in this respect: partisanship itself, not the sociological basis for it, conditions attitudes toward defense.

Table 5.20 also provides data regarding the influence of party affiliation on what is desired in terms of security arrangements by the Italians, Belgians, and Dutch. In Italy and Belgium, NATO does not fare well even among the conservative, liberal, and socialist parties, and, not surprisingly, much worse among Italian communist (PCI) adherents (12 percent). For the latter, accommodation with the Soviet Union ranks higher (14 percent), while the main preference is an independent West European force not allied to the United States (32 percent). For the followers of the other parties in the two

**TABLE 5.20: Preferred Security Arrangement by Political Party Supported, April 1980 (percent)**

Question: Thinking now of the protection of (SURVEY COUNTRY) against possible attack from the outside, which one of the statements listed on this card comes closest to your own view on how (SURVEY COUNTRY) would provide for its security in the 1980s (SHOW CARD I)?

| | Germany | | | Italy | | | | Belgium | | | Netherlands | | |
|---|---|---|---|---|---|---|---|---|---|---|---|---|---|
| | CDU/ CSU | FDP | SPD | DC[a] | PSI[b] | PCI[c] | | PVV/ PLP[d] | CVP/ PSC[e] | BSP/ PSB[f] | VVD[g] | CDA[h] | PVDA[i] |
| Number of cases | 351 | 46 | 419 | 346 | 106 | 149 | | 56 | 184 | 102 | 106 | 245 | 268 |
| The NATO alliance among the countries of Western Europe and the United States | 58 | 57 | 43 | 28 | 26 | 12 | | 21 | 35 | 31 | 58 | 44 | 32 |
| An independent West European defense force under European command, but allied to the United States | 16 | 15 | 24 | 40 | 31 | 10 | | 44 | 33 | 20 | 28 | 35 | 24 |

118

|  | 1 | 2 | 3 | 4 | 5 | 6 | 7 | 8 | 9 | 10 | 11 | 12 |
|---|---|---|---|---|---|---|---|---|---|---|---|---|
| An independent West European defense force under European command, but not allied to the United States | 5 | 9 | 12 | 9 | 24 | 32 | 9 | 7 | 14 | 1 | 5 | 10 |
| Rely on our own nation's defense force without belonging to any military alliance | 4 | 9 | 5 | 9 | 17 |  | 2 | 1 | 7 | 4 | 3 | 6 |
| Reduce our defense forces and rely on greater accommodation with the Soviet Union | 1 | 2 | 4 | 1 | 0 | 14 | 9 | 2 | 7 | 3 | 3 | 11 |
| Don't know | 15 | 9 | 13 | 17 | 10 | 14 | 16 | 22 | 23 | 8 | 10 | 17 |
| Total | 99 | 101 | 101 | 100 | 100 | 99 | 101 | 100 | 102 | 102 | 100 | 100 |

[a] Christian Democrats
[b] Italian Socialist Party
[c] Italian Communist Party
[d] Party of Liberty and Progress
[e] Christian Social Party
[f] Socialist Party
[g] Party of Freedom and Democracy
[h] Christian Democratic Appeal
[i] Labour Party

Source: USICA, *Research Memorandum*, December 4, 1980.

countries, such an independent force, but one allied with the United States, is generally the preferred security arrangement. In the Netherlands, NATO ranks highest among all major parties; it should be noted, however, that 11 percent of adherents of the Labor Party opted for accommodation of the Soviet Union.

## THE PROGRESSION OF WESTERN EUROPE'S PUBLIC OPINION PATTERN

The assessment presented here of the Eurodove sentiment in Western Europe based on 1980 data is consistent with subsequent data from secondary sources collected mostly in the first four months of 1981.

Eurodove attitudes are strengthened by widespread perceptions in Western Europe that Soviet aggression or political intimidation of West European governments (that is, Soviet pressure to adopt policies that are chiefly in the interest of the USSR) are not likely to occur in the foreseeable future. Majorities in West Germany, the Netherlands, and Norway expressed these views in March 1981; in France and Britain, opinion was about evenly divided on this issue.

Two points of political significance should be mentioned in this connection: first, in France, concern about a Soviet attack doubled from 1979 to 1981 (from 22 to 46 percent); second, the best-educated are considerably less concerned about a Soviet threat than the rest of the public—except in France, where the situation is reversed. Finally, for a small minority of West Europeans (about 10 percent), the planned long-term buildup of U.S. military forces constituted the foremost danger to their country.[14] At the same time, this building has somewhat attenuated West European expectations of the U.S. decline of military prowess as the proportion declined of those who saw the Soviets militarily ahead in five years (see Figure 5.3). This reversal of perceptions in 1981 was more pronounced among the best-educated than among the general public. A similar trend can be seen with respect to perceptions of U.S.-Soviet influence in world affairs in the future. The proportion of those attributing greater influence to the Soviet Union in five years declined, while perceptions ascribing greater world influence to the United States remained the same (see Figure 5.4).[15]

Whatever the perceptions about the consequences of the U.S. military buildup, there is a widespread desire in Western Europe to stay out of superpower disputes. This most likely reflects the conviction that superpower disputes constitute a serious threat to Western Europe's own security. In March 1981 such beliefs were reflected by large proportions of the public in Britain (41 percent) and in France (32 percent). These sentiments strengthen inclinations toward neutralism; indeed, in March 1981, 40 percent of the

## FIGURE 5.3: Expected Shifts in Military Balance, March-April 1981

| | USSR Ahead | US Ahead | Equal | Don't Know |
|---|---|---|---|---|
| **UK** | | | | |
| now | 52 | 11 | 27 | 11 |
| in 5 years | 30 | 20 | 27 | 22 |
| **FRANCE** | | | | |
| now | 30 | 16 | 38 | 16 |
| in 5 years | 17 | 17 | 28 | 37 |
| **FRG** | | | | |
| now | 33 | 18 | 33 | 14 |
| in 5 years | 27 | 16 | 31 | 26 |
| **NETHERLANDS** | | | | |
| now | 29 | 10 | 43 | 19 |
| in 5 years | 17 | 14 | 39 | 30 |
| **NORWAY** | | | | |
| now | 33 | 16 | 38 | 13 |
| in 5 years | 22 | 22 | 36 | 20 |

Source: Kenneth P. Adler and Douglas A. Wertman, "West European Security Concerns for the Eighties: Is NATO in Trouble?" Paper presented at the 1981 Annual Meeting of the American Association of Public Opinion Research at Buck Hill, Pa., May 28-31, 1981.

French respondents wanted France to become a neutral country, and similar feelings were expressed by 20 percent of the British respondents.[16] According to a survey by the German Allensbach Institute in 1980, one-third of the West German public felt it would be better to be "neutral like Switzerland" than to "belong to the Western defense alliance."[17]

Tendencies toward Eurodove attitudes and neutralism are reflected also in West European perceptions about the deployment of U.S. long-range theater nuclear forces in various European countries. Support for such deployment among West Europeans is relatively low. In Britain, during an April 1981 survey, 51 percent of the respondents were opposed to the stationing of cruise missiles on British soil, and 48 percent opposed the introduction of the neutron bomb into Europe. In Germany the opposition was 60 percent, in the Netherlands 50 percent, and in Belgium 42 percent. Most West Europeans are anxious to see new arms control negotiations initiated by the United States, both with respect to a new round of strategic arms limitation talks and especially regarding the deployment of LRTNF weapons by the Soviet Union and the United States.[18] Beyond that, there is a movement in Britain for unilateral nuclear disarmament, sponsored mostly by elements of the British Labour

## FIGURE 5.4: Influence of United States and Soviet Union on World Events, March-April 1981

| | USSR More Influence | US More Influence | Equal | Don't Know |
|---|---|---|---|---|
| **UK** | | | | |
| now | 29 | 21 | 39 | 10 |
| in 5 years | 20 | 22 | 30 | 28 |
| **FRANCE** | | | | |
| now | 25 | 18 | 44 | 13 |
| in 5 years | 10 | 18 | 36 | 36 |
| **FRG** | | | | |
| now | 22 | 21 | 38 | 19 |
| in 5 years | 16 | 22 | 35 | 26 |
| **NETHERLANDS** | | | | |
| now | 21 | 20 | 42 | 17 |
| in 5 years | 12 | 18 | 36 | 35 |
| **NORWAY** | | | | |
| now | 20 | 26 | 39 | 14 |
| in 5 years | 11 | 27 | 35 | 28 |

Source: Kenneth P. Adler and Douglas A. Wertman, "West European Security Concerns for the Eighties: Is NATO in Trouble?" Paper presented at the 1981 Annual Meeting of the American Association of Public Opinion Research at Buck Hill, Pa., May 28-31, 1981.

Party, with 23 percent of the British public in favor of such a move in April 1981. In the Netherlands, opinion was evenly divided on the general question of whether Western Europe should possess nuclear weapons.[19]

Considering the above expressions of selected segments of the West European public, it is not surprising that detente continues to hold considerable attraction for most West Europeans in spite of the Soviet invasion of Afghanistan and continuing threats of the USSR becoming involved in Poland. A survey by the German Allensbach Institute in January 1980 revealed that 74 percent of the respondents expressed the view that Germany should continue the policy of detente in the future (little difference in that issue by various age groups), and 53 percent thought that the West and East could peacefully coexist.[20] Consistent with these views, majorities in West Germany (67 percent) and France (52 percent) favored a conciliatory approach toward the Soviet Union; 65 percent of the West Germans as well as 54 percent of the French believed that the West had benefited as much from detente as had the Soviet Union. In contrast, a majority of Americans (57 percent) commended a policy of firmness vis-à-vis the Soviet Union; only 34 percent thought that the West had the same share of benefits from detente as had the USSR.[21]

## CONCLUSIONS

The data presented in this and the preceding chapters reveal the wide perceptional gaps that separate many West Europeans from Americans regarding security matters and East-West relations. Eurodoves seem to be gaining on Eurohawks while, in the United States, the prevailing views reflect firmness in dealing with the Soviet Union and a strong commitment to NATO with support for increased defense spending. On the other hand, in Western Europe support for NATO appears to be slipping somewhat, substantial opposition to increases in defense spending signifies that there is little interest in comprehensive sharing of the financial burden with the United States, and development of U.S. cruise missiles and other LRTNF weapons in Western Europe has only limited support among its population.

It is interesting to note that perceptions in Europe and the United States regarding the various security and East-West issues are not significantly influenced by the ages of the respondents.[22] In other words, younger and older people express similar views. On the other hand, it is most significant for the assessment of European public opinion that, as Adler and Wertman point out, the deployment of LRTNF weapons and the broader issue of how best to avoid involvement in war are issues that have become enmeshed in domestic politics.[23] As a consequence, these issues could have considerable influence on national policymakers whose decisions may be at cross-purposes with what the U.S. government wants to achieve. These decisions may not break up the Atlantic alliance, but if tendencies toward neutrality or a purely European defense force intensify, they may well weaken the overall structure of the common defense as a result of lowered European financial and material commitments. It is difficult to judge how much this trend could be countered by U.S. strengthening of its nuclear and conventional armaments, but unless European desires for meaningful negotiations on arms control between the superpowers are satisfied, the Atlantic "house" may eventually crumble. Hence, there is a need to examine in some detail the policy implications of an emerging dissension among the NATO countries. This will be the subject of Chapter 6.

## NOTES

1. Werner J. Feld and John K. Wildgen, *Domestic Political Realities and European Unification* (Boulder, Colo.: Westview Press, 1976).

2. Much of the philosophy behind USICA polls can be found in Charles Backstrom and Gerald Hursh-Cesar, *Survey Research*, 2d ed. (New York: John Wiley, 1971). Hursh-Cesar is acting director of the USICA.

3. U.S. Arms Control and Disarmament Agency, *World Military Expenditures and Arms Transfers, 1969-1978* (Washington, D.C., 1980).

4. Kenneth P. Adler and Douglas A. Wertman, "West European Security Concerns for the Eighties: Is NATO in Trouble?" Paper presented at the 1981 Annual Meeting of American Association for Public Opinion Research at Buck Hill, Pa., May 28-31, 1981, Table 5.

5. Translation provided by French Embassy Press and Information Service, *Statements from France*, 81 (June 1981): 3-4.

6. USICA, Briefing Paper on West European Public Opinion Regarding NATO, December 3, 1980.

7. See *Time*, July 6, 1981, pp. 22-24; and *New York Times*, July 5, 1981, p. 53.

8. USICA, Research Memorandum, "Whither Western Europe," April 9, 1981, p. 5.

9. Carl von Clausewitz, *On War*, ed. and trans. by Michael Howard and Peter Paret (Princeton, N.J.: Princeton University Press, 1976), pp. 86-87, emphasis in original.

10. Ibid.

11. Edward N. Luttwak, "On the Meaning of Strategy . . . for the United States in the 1980s," in *National Security in the 1980s: From Weakness to Strength*, ed. W. Scott Thompson (San Francisco: Institute for Contemporary Studies, 1980), p. 260.

12. Dennis Kavanagh, "Political Culture in Great Britain: The Decline of Civic Culture," in *The Civic Culture Revisited*, eds. Gabriel A. Almond and Sidney Verba (New York: Little, Brown, 1980), p. 170.

13. Adler and Wertman, in "West European Security," p. 17, point out that in other countries of Western Europe age group differences, at least, also show little influence on responses regarding security issues.

14. Ibid., pp. 2-3.

15. Ibid., p. 5.

16. USICA, Briefing Paper on West European Perceptions of the Soviet Threat, April 10, 1981.

17. Cited by Adler and Wertman, "West European Security," p. 8, who report that neutralist sentiment may be highest in Greece (50 percent in 1980), which may have changed after Greece's return to NATO. See also *The Allensbach Report*, 1980, E/4.

18. USICA, Briefing Paper regarding West European Views on TNF, April 1, 1981.

19. Adler and Wertman, "West European Security," p. 16.

20. *The Allensbach Report*, 1980, E/4.

21. USICA, Research Memorandum, "West European Key Security Issues," April 9, 1981.

22. Adler and Wertman, "West European Security," p. 18.

23. In this connection, see also Stephen F. Szabo, "The Successor Generation: Perception of Post War German Generation of the U.S. and the USSR." Paper presented at the 1980 Annual Meeting of the Southern Political Science Association, Atlanta, Ga., November 6-8, 1980. He stated as a tentative conclusion that "Generations appears to be a variable with some independent explanatory impact."

# 6

# POLICY IMPLICATIONS

## THE LINKAGE BETWEEN PUBLIC OPINION AND POLICY

Any assessment of the impact that the public opinion data presented in Chapters 4 and 5 may have on the formation and implementation of foreign and domestic policies in the NATO member states requires one to raise caution flags with respect to the causality between perceptions, attitudes, behavior, and policy actions. This problem area was touched on in Chapter 1, but it should be stressed again that the path from expression of public opinion on issues relevant to Atlantic defense and NATO to final decisions on what policies individual governments formulate or how they will implement them is long, arduous, and far from predictable.

The views expressed by respondents depend on many factors including the images formed over a period of time, their belief systems, their experiences, and the phrasing of particular questions, as well as how they are presented by the interviewer. Images are normally hard to change unless new information received is highly persuasive. It is easier to reject new information because by so doing one avoids having to change one's attitude. Even if a person recognizes that the new information is clearly discrepant with the image held and present beliefs, the validity of the information is doubted or it is interpreted in such a way as to obviate a change in attitude.[1] Hence, evoking a strong Soviet threat of a possible attack on Western Europe may reinforce the already existing anti-Soviet attitudes of most Americans, but it is likely to be rejected by many Europeans because it does not fit into their images and belief systems. After all, the shocks of the Soviet invasions of Czechoslovakia in 1968 and Afghanistan in 1979 were rather short-lived.

Perceptions and attitudes may be translated into corresponding behavior manifested by large-scale demonstrations and lobbying of varying intensity to influence national legislators and administrators in the direction of the views expressed by different publics. The intensity of the demonstrations staged in support of particular views depends to a large extent on the emotional content of the attitudes held that reflect these views. The demonstrations in West Germany, Great Britain, and the Netherlands against the stationing of new American TNF weapons in these countries fall into the category of high emotionalism, which in West Germany infected even some members of the army who participated actively in these demonstrations.[2] The strong emotional content of these views reflected in the demonstrations stems largely from a growing pacifist trend that was also evident among the 120,000 delegates at the National Congress of Evangelical Churches in Hamburg in spring 1981. The desire for peace is thus related to Christian imperatives. Under these circumstances, it is doubtful that official U.S. demands that the Germans cool their disputes about nuclear weapons and relations with the Soviet Union will be heeded.[3] Indeed, some Germans may resent such actions by the State Department as unwarranted interference in West German affairs.

The effectiveness of demonstrations and lobbying actions on behalf of particular views regarding foreign policy and security issues also depends on the degree to which domestic politics are involved. Especially, the more that economic issues are affected by pursuing one or the other course advocated by contending views and attitudes expressed in public opinion, the more sensitive governmental leaders will be to the public's voices in their decision-making on formulation and implementation of foreign and security policies. When questions of exports, jobs, social services, and the consequent distribution of governmental expenditures to either domestic or security needs are involved, domestic political concerns may well be ranked higher ultimately than immediate security demands.

These rather general considerations, however, are not intended to suggest that NATO country governments automatically follow the wishes of majorities or strong minorities when decisions on these views or objectives are likely to bring into play domestic political concerns regarding electoral politics and the future retention or loss of governmental power. Nevertheless, since proper responses by national governments to strongly perceived economic problems lie at the heart of the political process in all democracies, domestic politics cannot be ignored in the making of foreign and security policies. Obviously, the parameters of domestic politics vary among the NATO countries.

Whether and how much expression of public opinion actually becomes policy or influences the final policy decisions in concrete situations rests largely with the foreign policy and security policymaking processes which in themselves are highly intricate and differ from country to country. Policy positions or policy changes desired by substantial minorities (or even majorities) must run the gamut of organizations, especially the foreign and defense ministries, as well as other agencies that participate in the making of foreign and security policies, and the bureaucracies involved in the decisionmaking exercise. Using Graham Allison's terminology,[4] from the perspective of the "organizational process" model of foreign policymaking, the interests, organizational goals, and standard operating procedures of a number of ministries come into play and might promote or impede the desired positions or changes in the country's policies. From the perspective of Allison's "bureaucratic politics" model, officials involved in the formulation and implementation of relevant policies will inject the promotion of their own personal interests, including the expansion of their positions of power and prestige, as important guides and motivations in the policymaking process. This also brings up again the issues of images, belief systems, and experiences of the officials concerned with the policymaking process and the difficulty of attitude modification discussed earlier. Some of these officials may be sympathetic with or even fully supportive of particular public opinion views and attitudes, and others may be neutral or opposed. Hence direction in policy development will vary according to which attitudes are held by the officials concerned with particular proposals for policy positions or changes as these proposals make their way up the bureaucratic ladder toward the final decisions by governmental leaders in different NATO countries. It is on this level that electoral politics will have their greatest influence. It is only in final decisions (regarding both policy formulation and implementation) that the degree of influence that public opinion has exerted can be fully determined. Thus the prediction of linkage between public opinion and policymaking is uncertain. Nevertheless, it is fair to assume that, under conditions of high issue sensitivity to domestic and especially electoral politics, this linkage is likely to be established.

## NATO POLICIES UNDER DISAPPROVAL

In May 1977 the governments of the NATO member states reached an agreement to maintain a real yearly increase of 3 percent in defense expenditures. The reason for this commitment was the shift in the balance of power between NATO and the Warsaw Pact organization in favor of the latter, primarily due to the steady improvement of Soviet nuclear and conventional capabilities and a decline in the aggregate military strength of NATO. While these developments were solid reasons for the commitment for increased defense expenditure, the data in Chapter 5 clearly indicate that increases in defense spending had little support in France and West Germany or in the smaller NATO countries. Only in Britain was increased defense spending relatively popular in 1979 and early 1980, but by 1981 this popularity had vanished and a majority of the British respondents opposed increases in defense expenditures.[5]

Table 6.1 suggests that the policies of most European NATO allies in meeting their commitments, with few exceptions, gradually converged with public opinion during 1979 and 1980. While in 1978 a substantial number of European NATO countries achieved their commitments, in 1979 and 1980 only Britain and France were able to do so. (The 1980 figure for Luxembourg is meaningless since its armed forces are miniscule, totaling no more than 1,000 men.) European officials tend to regard the figures shown in this table as the maximum obtainable within which any future requirements must fit. If future economic trends remain poor, several NATO governments have warned that defense needs cannot be insulated from general cuts in overall expenditures.[6]

**TABLE 6.1: Percentage Change in NATO Defense Spending from Previous Year in Constant Prices**

| Country | 1978 | 1979 | 1980 |
|---|---|---|---|
| Belgium | 6.7 | 4.5 | −2.0[a] |
| Britain | −0.3 | 3.9 | 3.2 |
| Canada | −.2 | .9 | 3.4 |
| Denmark | 3.1 | .2 | −.6 |
| France | 4.9[b] | 3.0[b] | 3.5[b] |
| West Germany | 3.0 | 2.0 | 1.0[c] |
| Greece | −3.2[b] | .5[b] | NA |
| Italy | 3.2 | .8 | 3 |
| Luxembourg | 7.9 | 1.4 | 17.3 |
| Netherlands | −5.3 | 3.5 | 2.1 |
| Norway | 7.7 | 2.8 | 2.3[a] |
| Portugal | 1.7 | 12.3 | NA |
| Turkey | 0 | 2.1 | 2.1 |
| United States | 1.5[d] | 3.2[d] | 3.2[d] |
| non-United States NATO | 2.1 | 2.7 | 2.0 |

[a]These countries have informally indicated that their growth for 1980 may be better than depicted here.

[b]DOD estimate.

[c]FRG officials have confirmed that the Federal Republic will achieve the 3 percent commitment for 1980.

[d]These figures are based on the NATO definition of defense spending, which includes certain expenditures beyond those of the Department of Defense (for example, DOT expenditures for the Coast Guard and DOE spending for nuclear weapons). Based on the DOD definition of defense spending, the current estimate of U.S. real growth is 0.7 percent, 3.9 percent, and 2 percent for 1978, 1979, and 1980, respectively.

NA: Not available.

Source: "NATO After Afghanistan," report by the Subcommittee on Europe and the Middle East, U.S. House of Representatives, October 27, 1980, p. 46.

Concern with economic problems and unwillingness to cut spending for social services are also motivations for low public opinion support for increases in defense spending. Other reasons are likely to be low Soviet threat perceptions, preferences for detente and arms control negotiations, and a feeling that the United States' interest in protecting Western Europe will ultimately induce the U.S. government to bail out West European governments that lag in these defense expenditures.

Another NATO policy under fire relates to the deployment of long-range theater nuclear forces. In December 1979 the NATO member governments decided to upgrade and strengthen their arsenals of tactical nuclear weapons in Western Europe by deploying, beginning with 1983, Pershing II missiles and cruise missiles to counter the rapid expansion of SS-20 Soviet missiles, which are capable of hitting any target in Western Europe. Together with the increase in Backfire bombers and a new generation of Soviet long-range fighter bomber aircraft, the theater balance in Europe had been shifted heavily in favor of the Warsaw Pact organization.[7] It is important to note that the NATO decision for the deployment of advanced LRTNF weapons designed to restore the theater nuclear balance was linked to the initiation of arms control negotiations on all nuclear forces in Europe and, thereby, constituted a "dual track" policy. For the Europeans, the commitment to the pursuit of meaningful arms control negotiations is an indispensable concomitant to measures of defense.

The new U.S. missiles are scheduled to be installed in the United Kingdom, West Germany, and Italy, whose governments agreed to this move. Belgium and the Netherlands, which were also to be candidates for the initial deployment of the missiles, while endorsing the decision to upgrade and modernize tactical nuclear weapons in Europe, expressed reservations. Belgium finally gave qualified approval in September 1980, but the Netherlands wanted to wait two years before making a definite commitment. Both countries were anxious to see how the arms control negotiations were going to evolve.[8]

As indicated in Chapter 5, public opinion has expressed itself negatively regarding the installation of the LRTNF weapons in all countries earmarked for deployment except Italy, for which data so far are not available. As mentioned earlier, in some of these countries, especially West Germany, impressive demonstrations took place to protest as strongly as possible the stationing of these weapons on home soil. Many adherents of the Social Democratic Party in Germany, mostly those leaning to the left, have joined the opposition against the nuclear weapons. The issue has caused political difficulties for Chancellor Helmut Schmidt, who, with his foreign minister Hans Dietrich Genscher, has steadfastly supported the NATO policy on the deployment of the LRTNF forces. Indeed, Schmidt threatened to resign if his party would not back him on this issue. Nevertheless, large elements of the SPD, particularly those whose avowed creed is detente, rebel against the NATO policy and have joined ideologically the forces identified with the renascent pacifism of the churches, youth organizations, and environmentalist movements. Anti-capitalist sentiments have also come to the fore again with the SPD, and the political situation is aggravated by West Germany's 1.2 million unemployed.[9] Thus electoral politics are coming into play, and the political future of Helmut Schmidt may be jeopardized by this highly emotion-laden issue. Much may depend on the promised arms control negotiations to which the chancellor hopefully referred in a television interview on July 19, 1981.[10] If these negotiations should not make much progress by the end of 1982, Schmidt may well be compelled to repudiate the 1979 commitment regarding the deployment of LRTNF forces or be forced out of office.

## DIVISIVE ISSUES

To better understand the consequences of the perceptual gap separating West European and American publics for policy developments on both sides of the Atlantic, it is useful to review the issue areas that display the most serious cleavages and that, at the same time, are of particular import for the maintenance of Atlantic defense and East-West relations. Into this category clearly falls the question of how great the financial contribution to the common defense by the various NATO allies should be.

### The Problem of Burden Sharing

Americans are much more inclined to follow the lead of the government to increase spending on armaments and military personnel than West Europeans. While the commitments of most European governments to raise their financial contribution to NATO are attacked and the majority of the public opts for keeping spending at current levels, most Americans accept the increases. This disparity in views is likely to create in American minds the impression of unfairness because the burden of defense, which is designed to produce definite benefits for all (although their form may vary from country to country), should be shared as equally as possible. Considering the tremendous economic progress made by most of the European allies in the 1960s and the 1970s, the remarks made on burden sharing in 1972 by McGeorge Bundy, National Security Advisor in the Kennedy administration, remain valid today:

> It is a fact of life for both Europe and the United States that your "resolutely amilitary" population depends for its peace of mind, at least in part, upon the fact that *our* population is prepared to pay twice as much of its national income for the common defense. I do not lament this expense. I think that in the main it is essential for our own security, and that we should save very few dollars if there were no Europe for us to help defend. Moreover

> I recognize that much has already been done, and that more can reasonably be predicted, in the way of burden-sharing. Nonetheless, I think it would be asking a great deal of my fellow citizens, and even more of their elected representatives, to expect them to neglect entirely, in the reconstruction of the economic and financial foundations that are indispensable to all of us, the fact that among the open societies of the North Atlantic and Pacific, there is one which does much more than the others to provide for a defense which is still common.[11]

Americans should not be under any illusion that the burden-sharing situation, a troublesome problem of long-standing, is likely to be fully resolved to the satisfaction of the U.S. government in the foreseeable future. Clear-cut comparisons between the defense expenditures of the NATO allies are difficult because of differences in the size of countries as well as in the nature and shape of their economies. Nevertheless, the data for 1978 regarding defense expenditures of NATO countries (which were presented in Figure 5.1) show substantial disparities despite the fact that British and French percentages of defense expenditures related to GNP are the highest in Europe. On the other end of the spectrum are Luxembourg, Italy, and Denmark, which showed the lowest percentages, 1.1, 2.4, and 2.4 percent, respectively.[12]

The governments of the European NATO countries have some potent arguments to justify their lower financial contributions to the common defense. They point out that in times of rampant inflation, stagnant growth, and very high energy costs, their highest priority is to preserve the health of their economies, which is essential for their political stability. They also want, naturally, to avoid electoral defeat by their political opponents, some of whom have opposed NATO over the years. As already mentioned in Chapter 5, they stress that they provide a larger share—over 75 percent—of the ground and air forces for the defense of Europe than does the United States and Canada. Finally, they emphasize that most of the European allies use conscription for the manpower needed in their military establishments, while Americans employ an all-volunteer force that is very expensive and skirts thereby the equal responsibility and the many hardships to which young Europeans are subjected.[13]

Does the United States have any leverage that would compel the European member governments of NATO to adjust their defense policies in accordance with U.S. goals and wishes? A substantial part of American opinion holds that greater burden sharing by all NATO allies should be a precondition for additional defense contributions by the United States, with GNP per capita to be the criterion for the allies' share. Others believe that the United States should withdraw two or more divisions now stationed in Europe, requiring the Europeans to replace the manpower that would be lost.[14] This is basically the scheme that was proposed for many years by former Senator Mike Mansfield.

Both suggestions are counterproductive to U.S. goals and should be rejected. Given the mood of the Europeans as shown by the data presented in Chapter 5, especially their clear inclinations toward neutralism and perhaps pacifism, leverage employed by the United States may well drive more Europeans to accommodations with the Soviet Union than would be the case otherwise. Moreover, withdrawal of U.S. divisions would be military folly at a time when NATO forces should be strengthened rather than weakened. Such actions would send the wrong signals to friends as well as to adversaries. The reduction of U.S. forces would likely lead to similar actions by other NATO allies and thus would have effects contrary to those intended. On the other hand, moving forward with strengthening U.S. strategic and conventional forces may beget similar actions,[15] although such an outcome is far from certain.

**Commitment to NATO**

When attempting to assess differences in the commitment to NATO by the American and West European publics, it is necessary to take a careful look at how particular questions on this topic were phrased in the polls taken. In the United States, the question posed by the Gallup survey in 1980 was straightforward, asking respondents whether they would like to increase, decrease, or keep the same the U.S. commitment to NATO. An additional option was withdrawal. As Table 4.5 showed, about two-thirds of the respondents wanted either to increase or maintain this commitment. Strong U.S. support for NATO was also suggested in Table 4.4, which posed the same question in 1974 and 1978. The authors own survey of student opinions in the University of New Orleans reflected even greater support (see Table 3.5 and the analysis in Chapter 3).

The choices offered the West European respondents regarding their support of NATO were much more differentiated and were designed to tap their views on the best security arrangements for their country. Table 5.5 showed that NATO is most supported by the Germans (57.6 percent) as being the most desirable security arrangement, followed by the British (49.9 percent). The low French support is not only connected with latent Gaullism, but also with the fact that many French citizens do not have a clear understanding of France's relationship with NATO. From Table 5.20, which broke down desired security arrangements by party identification, one saw that NATO gets good marks by the Dutch, while only minorities in Italy and Belgium view NATO as the preferred security arrangement. While substantial minorities in all six countries consider the arrangement of an alliance between the United States and an independent West European defense force under European command as the most desirable defense arrangement, such an alliance would be structurally and functionally quite different from NATO and would reduce the leadership potential of the United States, which it can and does exercise in NATO. While from the American perspective any kind of Atlantic alliance might be preferable to an independent European force or to purely national forces, one must be aware that a Euro-U.S. alliance would result in a materially weaker defense posture than that provided by NATO. American public opinion, with its strong support for NATO, and the American media's concern for an effective NATO organization as a powerful bulwark of defense, would have difficulty comprehending European preferences for a Euro-U.S. alliance without NATO. While these preferences undoubtedly reflect the very understandable desires of many Europeans to have a larger voice in the defense of their own continent, they could also be interpreted as subtle indications of Eurodove sentiments inasmuch as they signify rejection of an organization that has been symbolizing tough military counteraction against Soviet encroachment. Obviously, the other choices—independent European or national defense forces and greater accommodation of the Soviet Union—are progressively stronger indications or Eurodove tendencies.

In a more recent poll (March 1981), one sees the trend toward security arrangements other than the existing NATO structure increasing. In this poll, the choice of a Euro-U.S. alliance was changed to a choice of a modified NATO structure in which Western Europe would have a greater voice but would also pay more for its cost, perhaps a very unrealistic scenario. In any case, only in Germany did NATO as currently constituted retain about the same majority support as in 1980. In Britain, France, and the Netherlands, support for NATO had eroded in 1981 (35, 10, and 31 percent, respectively). Even if the percentages for the old and the modified NATO are summed, they do not reach the level of support given to NATO plus a Euro-U.S. alliance in 1980.[16]

Another question asked in March 1981 in some European NATO countries was whether respondents still considered NATO "essential" to their country's security. Majorities in Britain, West Germany, Italy, Norway, and the Netherlands answered in the affirmative, although in Britain those answering in the affirmative declined from 79 percent in October 1980 to 70 percent in March 1981; in West Germany it declined from 88 percent to 62 percent.[17] Does the affirmation of NATO as "essential" mean necessary acceptance and support only for the present or also for the future, or do the preferences expressed for various security arrangements represent the better indicators of NATO support in the years to come and perhaps already now? The authors lean toward the latter interpretation of the available data, especially in the light of the downward trend of affirmative responses in Britain and Germany. This interpretation is also sustained by other tendencies toward Eurodove sentiments. The total trend picture of public opinion in Western Europe appears to be producing a widening gulf between the two sides of the Atlantic that eventually could endanger both NATO and Atlantic defense in general. United States defense policy is predicated upon a staunch NATO; if the

European NATO allies were to feel compelled in due time to respond favorably to the emerging trends in Western Europe, policies may be initiated by some of the NATO governments leading to serious friction and division within the Atlantic partnership. An alarmed American public may then clamor for a "fortress America" policy that would not only have serious security ramifications, but would also result in grave economic consequences on a global scale.

**The LRTNF Issue**

As indicated earlier in this chapter, the LRTNF issue is likely to have significant domestic political implications in the European NATO countries, especially in West Germany. Fears that the stationing of the new U.S. weapons might draw Western Europe into a war that might result in widespread destruction and misery, and serious apprehension that at a minimum the pursuit of detente, cherished by many Europeans as indispensable, would be impaired if not made impossible, make this issue potentially very divisive within NATO Europe and between the transatlantic partners. Rejection of these weapons by West European governments individually or collectively would be seen by a large segment of the American public as a clear indication of strong Eurodove sentiments and evidence that Europe was moving toward neutralism or even Finlandization. It would disillusion many in the United States who, perhaps not too well informed about happenings in Western Europe, had placed their trust in a strong Atlantic partnership. The level of transatlantic tensions would be raised materially, creating many dangers for the solidity of NATO and Atlantic defense.

**Detente**

The disparity of American and European views on the subject of detente was discussed in Chapter 5. Disagreements about the pursuit of detente began in the 1960s when many Europeans became persuaded that by a purposeful reduction of tensions in East-West relations, a stable and enduring peace could be gradually achieved. Indeed, detente became official NATO policy in 1967 when the NATO Council Report on the Future Tasks of the Alliance (the so-called Harmel Report) underlined the need to achieve a more stable relationship with Eastern Europe through a policy aimed at lessening tensions between East and West and progressively increasing areas of cooperation.[18] However, in the United States, detente was often looked upon with suspicion. It was seen as a scheme through which Soviet leaders were seeking to attain many objectives, such as the importation of high technology items and the extension of credits by Western financial institutions, which would shore up their lagging consumer economy and provide the Soviet Union with needed technology that its scientists had not been able to achieve by themselves. The end result would be to indirectly strengthen Soviet military capabilities. While the Soviet invasion of Czechoslovakia in 1968 temporarily cooled the fervor for detente, a few months after the invasion detente had regained its appeal, especially in Western Europe.

The Conference on Security and Cooperation in Europe (CSCE), which was held from July 1973 to August 1975 in Helsinki and Geneva and concluded with the signing of a document known as The Final Act by the governments of the participating countries, provided a formal framework for detente. The United States, which initially insisted on linking progress in the talks on mutual and balanced force reductions (MBFR) (also begun in 1973) with that on CSCE, later dropped its condition on linkage for the conclusion of the latter negotiations. During the U.S. presidential campaign in 1976, detente became a very controversial issue, and President Ford banned the use of the term in his campaign efforts. Earlier, in 1971 and 1972, President Nixon and Henry Kissinger had a much more positive view of detente and what it could accomplish.[19]

While the European NATO countries have had a rather consistent record of implementing detente policies, successive U.S. administrations have vacillated in their support of detente and have often seen it as a one-way street serving mostly Soviet interests. Clearly, the Reagan administration is very cautious in its approach to detente. As the summit meeting in Ottawa has shown, Reagan would like to restrict Western trade with the Soviet Union, especially as far as strategically valuable products for the Soviet military establishments are concerned. Hence there is no doubt that detente is potentially a divisive issue and, taken together with the other issues—burden sharing, the commitment to NATO, and the implementation of the LRTNF decision—illustrates the range of problems that policymakers on both sides of the Atlantic are likely to face in the early 1980s.

## TRANSATLANTIC POLICY DISPARITIES: ARE THERE ANY SOLUTIONS?

Although there is general recognition in all NATO countries of the rapid expansion of Soviet military might during the 1980s, perceptual differences about the meaning and consequences of this expansion exist among both the public and governments in these countries, as the discussion in this volume makes quite evident. Not surprisingly, the suggested policy responses to deal with the Soviet military buildup within the overall context of East-West relations have also differed appreciably and have been influenced by perceptions of the national interest in various NATO member states. The big question, then, is how can these different policy responses be reconciled and how can coordinated policies toward the Soviet Union be put in place.

Three important dimensions of the policy-coordinating process must be kept in mind. First, the strategic concerns of individual NATO partners are not the same. Second, the range and scope of economic interests as they relate to East-West problems differ from country to country. Third, domestic political interests, including electoral politics, are affected by governmental policy choices and, therefore per force, these interests influence which policies are chosen. On the other hand, it is precisely the interrelationship of these three dimensions that may provide opportunities for the coordination of policies and greater harmony among the NATO allies.

**Strategic Concerns**

No country is more exposed to the effects of Warsaw Pact aggression and Soviet political pressure than West Germany. At the same time, the division of Germany remains a festering sore in the minds of many Germans, although they realize that fully healing this sore cannot but be relegated to the distant future. The Basic Law of the Federal Republic of Germany, its constitution, exhorts all Germans to work for reunification. Hence, improving the relations between the people of the Federal Republic and the German Democratic Republic (East Germany) is a high priority. For this reason, pursuit of the *Ostpolitik*, initiated by former chancellor Willi Brandt, is seen by most Germans, including the present government of Helmut Schmidt, as an essential policy instrument to attain this goal.[20] The successful implementation of *Ostpolitik* requires the maintenance of a relatively harmonious relationship with the Soviet leadership which, in turn, fosters and strengthens tendencies toward detente and perhaps neutralism. West German opposition to being the only West European country to allow the stationing of U.S. LRTNF weapons on its soil is closely connected to its government's concern in the maintaining of good relations with Moscow. There is fear that in such an event these relations would seriously deteriorate, and that the Soviet Union might retaliate against the Federal Republic, in particular West Berlin.[21] On the other hand, the West Germans must realize that without a strong and cohesive NATO partnership they may have little leverage to extract even minimal concessions from Moscow. Perhaps for this reason, as well as to express loyalty to its express concurrence in 1979 to support the LRTNF modernization program, the West German government, backed overwhelmingly by the Bundestag, has reaffirmed its consent to the stationing of the new nuclear weapons in Europe.[22] However, the need for early arms control negotiations on this issue with Moscow has also been stressed again and again and seems to be taken seriously by the Reagan administration, although, if past experiences regarding negotiations with the Soviet Union are a guide, reaching any agreement may take several years.

Although Belgium and the Netherlands are geographically farther away from the threat of Soviet ground forces than is West Germany, their governments, as noted earlier, have backtracked somewhat from their 1979 commitment to allow stationing of LRTNF weapons on their soil. Indeed, the fragile and progressively eroding support of the two countries for theater nuclear force modernization stems less from strategic reasons than domestic political problems, as shall be seen later. Nevertheless, this development may have a snowballing adverse effect on the modernization effort as, for example, critical voices about LRTNF are also heard in Great Britain.

Only the United States has been steadfast in its intention to meet the Soviet threat with a comprehensive military buildup wherever needed in the world. The cost of the program, exceeding $1 trillion, is no deterrent, and increased military spending is backed by near-national consensus.[23]

## Economic Considerations

Perhaps nothing feeds tendencies toward detente more than economic considerations and incentives. Economic benefits in terms of increased job opportunities, improved trade and payments balances, and prospects for lower inflation exert powerful influences when it comes to formulating and implementing policies in an East-West context. Therefore trade with the Soviet Union and its East European satellites is seen as desirable by all NATO countries, albeit to varying degrees. Restrictions on this trade, even with respect to high technology products, tend to be resisted. During the Ottawa summit in July 1981, the United States pressed for such restrictions, but it is uncertain how far it was able to prevail. Obviously, Europeans may have looked upon these U.S. efforts with considerable suspicion, given the Reagan administration's flip-flop on wheat sales to the Soviet Union and current U.S. endeavors to push such sales as vigorously as possible.[24] Consistency in U.S. foreign policy remains an elusive virtue.

With the economic situation in Western Europe at present being much more precarious than in the United States, and unemployment, especially among the young seeking to enter the job market, rising dangerously, the Europeans must rely for their economic well-being much more on international trade than the United States, since traditionally exports have constituted a much larger share of their GNP than is the case in the United States. This factor and high dependence on foreign energy sources, far above that of the United States, have been major motivations for the planned participation of West Germany, Belgium, France, Italy, and the Netherlands in the construction of a 3,000-mile pipeline from Western Siberia to Western Europe that would be able to deliver some 40 billion cubic meters of natural gas annually. The West European participants in this $9.5 billion project hope to furnish much of the needed materials for this venture. West Germany will be providing the largest share of financing for construction of the pipeline and will also be the largest importer of gas once the system is operational.[25] An American firm, Caterpillar, is also among the suppliers of equipment for the project.

There are still hurdles to overcome before the pipeline becomes a reality. The Soviet Union claims that the interest rate charged for financing the project is too high, and agreement is lacking on the amount of gas to be delivered and what the price of the gas will be.

The U.S. government has expressed apprehension that the pipeline will make Western Europe dangerously dependent on the Soviet Union for energy supplies—a 30 percent dependence for Germany alone—and this view has won various degrees of support from the project partners. However, European trepidation has not led any of the participants to drop out of the project; rather, their will to persist in this venture has been voiced on several occasions. Only if Washington would take a very strong stand, including the revocation of export licenses for Caterpillar, is there a chance to persuade Germany and the other participants to desist from this venture. On the other hand, any improvement of the Afghan and Polish situations would accelerate progress toward a complete agreement between the Soviet Union and the Western participants.[26]

The unfavorable economic conditions in Western Europe may also have made the promised increase of 3 percent in national defense contributions obsolete. Even though German officials in 1980 promised this increase (see Table 6.1), 1981 may see an increase of only 2.2 percent, or perhaps none at all.

National economic interests of the European NATO partners have also made themselves felt in the organization's procurement programs. Concerns were expressed that too large a share of the weapons and equipment purchased for the allies came from the United States. A proposal was made to initiate a "two-way street" concept in the NATO procurement policies to provide greater opportunities for European producers and, thereby, expand the availability of jobs.[27] Although the aspirations of the Europeans have not been fully met, progress is being made toward a common transatlantic defense market.

Finally, North-South relations have economic and strategic implications that have a bearing also on East-West relations. The Europeans have been more sensitive to third world problems than has Washington because of their serious dependence on raw materials found in the third world, especially oil; the special economic and political relations of the European Community countries with Africa, through the Lomé Convention; and the needed markets that the less-developed areas provide for European products. Manifestations of Soviet expansionism in Africa and the Middle East (such as in Ethiopia, Angola, and

South Yemen) have heightened European concerns. Hence, the European allies have been more anxious to consider and meet the aspirations of third world leaders than has been the case with the United States. This was evident during the Ottawa summit when the European leaders insisted that the demands for global negotiations in the U.N. General Assembly on the implementation of the New International Economic Order be given a favorable response.

**Domestic Political Problems**

The data in Chapter 5 made it evident that party identification was an influential factor in various attitudes of the respondents regarding NATO. The potential impact of public opinion regarding emotion-laden issues on electoral politics and indirectly on possible policy choices was discussed earlier. The example used was German Chancellor Schmidt's problem with the left-leaning sector of the SPD membership, German adherents of pacifism, and the environmentalists.

Similar political problems are coming to light in other European NATO countries as well. In the Netherlands, the ruling coalition is made up of Christian Democratic parties and conservative Liberals. While the latter support the LRTNF weapons, the Christian Democrats, under pressure from antinuclear church groups, have put off the deployment decision until the end of 1981. The Labor Party, which might join the Christian Democrats in a new coalition government after the election in May 1982, also oppose the deployment. In Britain, as well as in other European countries, the antinuclear movement is growing in strength. Although this movement draws inspiration from the left, pacifist and religious organizations lend powerful support with the argument that nuclear weapons are morally abhorrent. The Soviet Union uses these arguments to campaign against NATO theater nuclear modernization in Western Europe. The tenet "better red than dead" seems to be spreading on the old continent.

A social-psychological factor with political overtones that is likely to have some bearing on policy choices, is the feeling of many Europeans that because of the United States' exclusive finger on the nuclear trigger, they have little say about their own destiny. Although representatives of the European allies are now participating in the targeting of U.S. strategic weapons through membership in NATO's Nuclear Planning Group, there remains widespread unhappiness with the limited role NATO Europe plays in the common defense. Resentment about the unequal influence that the United States and Western Europe have may reduce the sense of commitment of the public and governments to the Atlantic defense enterprise. Particularly in the smaller NATO member nations this state of affairs may generate sentiments of futility and create impressions that their contributions to the total NATO defense effort are unimportant and that they do not need to make sacrifices since they would hardly enhance NATO's overall capabilities.[28]

Of course, the U.S. government is also responsive to powerful political pressures. The lifting of the grain embargo by the Reagan administration to assure farmers' support for coming election campaigns is clear evidence of such responsiveness.

## POLICY COORDINATION AND RECONCILIATION

If a truly common Atlantic foreign policy could be formed across most issues facing the NATO member states, the problem of policy coordination would be solved. However, in spite of a comprehensive mechanism in place to coordinate the foreign policies of the member governments of the European Community, the so-called European Political Cooperation (EPC) scheme, the results have not been overwhelming.[29] Still, some successes have been recorded, for example, the common policies developed with respect to the negotiations leading to the signing of the CSCE Final Act in Helsinki and policy toward the Israeli-Arab conflict.

Interestingly, as Table 6.2 shows, the publics in most major NATO countries do not favor a common Atlantic foreign policy. West Germany is the exception. The British prefer an independent foreign policy, presumably the EPC system. It should be noted that the EC constituent treaties also provide selected instruments for foreign economic policies which, however, have not always been fully used by the EC member states.[30]

To solve the problems of attitudinal, interest, and policy disparities among the NATO allies, the direction of the major research institutes on foreign policy and international politics have issued a perceptive report entitled *Western Security: What Has Changed? What Should Be Done?*[31] This report analyzes the reasons for some of the problems plaguing the alliance and makes a number of recommendations. The main emphasis for bridging the gaps between NATO members is an improved consultation, including on third world problems related to East-West issues, and policy coordination. Of course, the lack of appropriate consultation within NATO has been deplored again and again over the last two decades, and still its systematic use remains elusive. Part of the problem is the absence of a clear concept of consultation and whether those consulted can have an expectation that their counsel will influence the forthcoming decision—if the decision has not already been made. This was the case when the United States ordered a worldwide alert of its armed forces during the 1973 Arab-Israeli war when the Israelis appeared to be near defeat and Washington was preparing to launch a rescue operation. The neutron warhead production decision by the Reagan administration is, as well, a model problem in defining consultation.

**TABLE 6.2: Preferred Foreign Policy Arrangement by Country, April 1980 (percent)**

Which of the following statements comes closest to your views of how (SURVEY COUNTRY) should conduct its foreign policy?

| | Belgium | FRG | France | Italy | Great Britain | Nether-lands | Weighted Average* |
|---|---|---|---|---|---|---|---|
| Make its own foreign policy decisions independent of other nations | 16 | 12 | 27 | 16 | 35 | 22 | 22 |
| Join with the other EEC member states to develop a common European Community foreign policy toward the rest of the world | 33 | 25 | 38 | 40 | 20 | 33 | 30 |
| Join with the other EEC member states and with the United States to develop a common Atlantic foreign policy | 19 | 37 | 11 | 25 | 28 | 25 | 25 |
| Join with the other EEC member states and with Eastern Europe and the Soviet Union to develop an all-European policy | 5 | 10 | 8 | 6 | 6 | 8 | 8 |
| Don't know | 27 | 16 | 16 | 13 | 11 | 12 | 15 |
| Total | 100 | 100 | 100 | 100 | 100 | 100 | 100 |

*Six-country average weighted to reflect population size.
Source: USICA, *Research Memorandum*, November 13, 1980, Table 3.

Undoubtedly, an improved consultation process will aid in the policy coordination of the NATO countries, but much more needs to be done to achieve this objective. According to the report:

> This includes a better management of alliance relations within NATO on East-West issues, and a transformation of the seven-nation summits to include political as well as economic issues. Most importantly, [there is need] for the creation of principal national groups to deal with particular problem areas in the Third World. These groups should be flexibly organized, consist of only those nations responsible for action, keep interested partners informed, maintain secrecy of discussions, and be visible in practice. The first such group, to be formed immediately, should be on the Gulf/South West Asia region and include the five principal nations—the United States, Britain, France, Germany and Japan.[32]

This is an ambitious program that, according to the authors of the report, will benefit both sides of the Atlantic. Within the framework of this program, Europe would assume greater responsibilities in dealing with the Soviet threat and in securing Western interests in the third world; in so doing it would acquire new influence over U.S. policy and gain more sensitive attention to its perspectives. The United States, through genuinely shared arrangements and joint decision-making, would elicit a greater European contribution, keyed not to placating Washington but to the pursuit of the West's common goals.[33]

How well this prescription for the solution of NATO's problems will work is difficult to predict. American perceptions of Western Europe sliding toward neutralism, pacifism, and Finlandization are widespread, especially among those now in charge of American foreign policymaking. The perceptions are in line with selected public opinion data according to which compromises with the Soviet Union and the continuation of detente are strongly favored.[34] In Europe, there is strong suspicion that Americans may aspire to return to the era of U.S. supremacy and absolute leadership in world affairs, a suspicion that finds easy confirmation in the smooth passage of a tremendously increased defense budget by Congress. These perceptions may be difficult to change. As Karl Deutsch and Richard Merritt have pointed out after undertaking a careful and detailed study regarding the effects of external events on attitudes and images, changes of images held by populations in most countries move at a glacial pace.[35] Hence, it is doubtful that the creation of new mechanisms for collective decisionmaking within the NATO community will by itself produce the necessary policy coordination to bridge the current gaps in attitudes and national policy inclinations displayed on both sides of the Atlantic.

The Reagan administration has not as yet gotten its act together for dealing with the Soviet Union and East-West relations. Policy inconsistencies as well as divergent and confusing rhetoric on the highest level have obscured, perhaps purposely, the aims of the administration. There has been concern about the absence of a clear policy in the United States despite national support for expanding the military establishment. Among the allies, President Mitterand expressed their anxiety when he remarked to James Reston of the *New York Times* that "there is no guiding thought," referring not only to the United States, but Europe as well.[36]

There seems little doubt that the United States is in the process of adopting a hard line toward the Soviet Union. This stand will be backed by a military buildup intended to give U.S. armed forces a slight strategic edge over the Soviet Union. President Reagan's decision in early August 1981 to move forward with the full production of the neutron weapon (a reversal of Carter's policy) is a clear indication of this intent. It is an attempt to counter quickly the superior military might of the Soviet bloc with its almost 3-to-1 advantage in tanks in central Europe. It also appears certain that a new round of SALT negotiations is envisioned once the U.S. government is able to deal with the USSR from a position of strength. However, reaching this stage in a realistic fashion may take years; in the meantime, the alliance, whose national constituencies may be influenced by accurate perceptions and downright illusions, suffers from growing disarray. Indeed, the *Economist*, certainly a responsible publication, characterized the alliance recently as being "in the early stages of what could be terminal illness."[37]

## SUGGESTIONS FOR THE FUTURE

The United States, as the foremost power in the alliance, must take timely, decisive steps to halt the disintegration of NATO. First, it must respond to European demands, especially those of Chancellor Schmidt, for an early initiation of talks with the Soviet Union on the LRTNF issue by giving specific dates when it is prepared to enter into meaningful negotiations.[38] As has already been mentioned, such negotiations have a way of starting very slowly, dealing initially only with procedures and the agenda. The Europeans need assurances that these talks will be pursued vigorously on the part of Washington so that some solution may be visible before the end of 1982. Of course, what the attitude of the Soviet Union will be in this connection cannot be predicted. It may want to engage in delays to intensify the disarray and disagreements among the NATO countries.

Second, the United States must be more forthcoming in economic matters, such as the problem of high interest rates that cause damage to European economies and about which many complaints were heard at the Ottawa summit. In the second half of the 1970s, Washington asked West Germany to accelerate its economy so it would serve as a "locomotive" to the economies of other Western countries. Despite misgivings, the federal government acceded, exposing itself to a higher inflation than would have been the case otherwise. There may be other instances where the economic interdependence linking the NATO countries can be used by Washington to shore up the alliance.

Although the Reagan administration is preoccupied at present with East-West relations, and perhaps rightly so, North-South relations also affect the economic interests of the United States. The United States should not ignore the great sensitivity many European NATO countries have about the demands of the third world, but rather should join them in finding solutions for the most serious difficulties many less-developed countries are facing. Although American policymakers oppose many aspects of the new international economic order, Washington does not want to be completely isolated when the global negotiations get under way in the U.N. General Assembly.

It is important that the military buildup of U.S. forces be seen by the world not as simply a tool of the United States to regain overwhelming influence in global affairs. Nor should the production of the neutron warhead be viewed as an attempt to limit nuclear war to Europe or to weaken the U.S. commitment to the employment of strategic nuclear weapons. Rather, it must be pointed out to the Europeans that this is an effort to strengthen both *their* and the U.S. defense against Soviet aggression or political encroachment and should deepen their confidence and trust in U.S. capabilities and resolve. If these notions can be successfully portrayed to NATO Europe, it may well be the means to counteract all Eurodove tendencies by building up again or reinforcing their confidence in themselves.

There are, as well, some measures that Europeans can take to hold up their end of the alliance while the United States looks to its diplomatic, economic, and military responsibilities toward Europe. Here we are not speaking of weapons purchases or anything to do with the hardware of defense. Rather, we want to emphasize the notion of perceptions, the software of the Western alliance. It is time that more European politicians display toward American public opinion the kind of sensitivity they regularly demand from American leaders. We have seen an example of this in French Foreign Minister Claude Cheysson's remarks (Ch. 5).

It needs to be understood in Europe that Americans are not very Rousseauvian in international politics—especially since Viet Nam. That is, Americans are not inclined to force people to be free. Should the widespread loathing for America and things American, typical of many European intellectuals and journalists, become more widely known in the United States, and should it be considered representative of European opinion generally, there would be calls for reexamination of the U.S. commitment to Europe. This would simply involve the two continents in a vicious circle and erode the moral basis of the alliance. This would intensify American tendencies toward an island-nation mentality with a fortress-like foreign policy reminiscent of the isolationism of a generation or so ago. An isolated United States could not help but be an encouragement to Soviet imperialism.

These suggestions may not be sufficiently comprehensive to completely halt NATO's spreading cancer, but they may constitute the beginning of a return to full health by the patient. NATO has successfully maintained the peace for more than three decades and has assured the security of Western Europe, Canada, and the United States. It is hoped that circumspect and resolute policies, especially by the United States but by the European allies as well, will enable NATO to assure peace for many more decades to come.

## NOTES

1. For a more detailed discussion of attitude preservation and change, see Robert Jervis, *Perceptions and Misperceptions in International Politics* (Princeton, N.J.: Princeton University Press, 1976), pp. 291-97.
2. See *Facts on File*, April 10, 1981, p. 246; and *New York Times*, April 8, 1981.
3. The *Times-Picayune–States-Item* (New Orleans), June 30, 1981.
4. Graham T. Allison, "Conceptual Models and the Cuban Missile Crisis," in *Readings on American Foreign Policy: A Bureaucratic Perspective*, eds. Morton H. Halperin and Arnold Kantor (Boston: Little, Brown, 1973), pp. 45-83.
5. See Table 5.9 in the preceding chapter and Table 5 in Kenneth P. Adler and Douglas A. Wertman, "West European Security Concerns for the Eighties: Is NATO in Trouble?" Paper presented at the 1981 Annual Meeting of American Association for Public Opinion Research at Buck Hill, Pa., May 28-31, 1981.
6. Committee on Foreign Affairs, U.S. House of Representatives, "NATO After Afghanistan," report prepared for the Subcommittee on Europe and the Middle East, October 27, 1980, p. 13.
7. For an up-to-date discussion of the balance of strategic and tactical nuclear weapons in East-West relations, see the Atlantic Council of the United States, *The Credibility of the NATO Deterrent* (Washington, D.C., 1981).
8. "NATO After Afghanistan," p. 19.
9. *Frankfurter Allgemeine Zeitung*, June 4, 1981.
10. ABC Television, *Issues and Answers*, July 19, 1981.
11. *Europe Documents*, No. 710, December 14, 1972.
12. "NATO After Afghanistan," Table 3, p. 44.
13. *The Credibility of the NATO Deterrent*, pp. 40-41.
14. Ibid., p. 41.
15. Ibid.
16. For details of this poll see Adler and Wertman, "West European Security," Table 4.
17. Ibid., p. 6 and Table 3.
18. NATO Information Service, *NATO Handbook* (Brussels, 1980), p. 24.
19. See Henry Kissinger, *White House Years* (Boston: Little, Brown, 1979), pp. 949, 964.
20. See *Relay from Bonn*, "The Week in Germany," June 19, 1981.
21. Institute for Foreign Policy Analysis, *Fourth German-American Roundtable on NATO* (1981), p. 8.
22. *Hannoversche Allgemeine*, May 27, 1981.

23. See also *Time*, June 1, 1981, p. 12; and July 27, 1981, p. 9.
24. *Times-Picayune–States-Item* (New Orleans), July 25, 1981.
25. For details see *World Business Weekly*, June 29, 1981, pp. 15-16.
26. Ibid.
27. For a full discussion of this issue see Eugene J. Megaros, "NATO Europe and the United States: The Two-Way Street Concept," in *Western Europe's Global Reach*, ed. Werner J. Feld (New York: Pergamon Press, 1980), pp. 233-54.
28. Adler and Wertman, "West European Security," p. 12.
29. For details see Wolfgang Wessels, "New Forms of Foreign Policy Formulation in Western Europe," in *Western Europe's Global Reach*, ed. Werner J. Feld (New York: Pergamon Press, 1980), pp. 12-29.
30. See Werner J. Feld, *The European Community in World Affairs* (Sherman Oaks, Calif.: Alfred Publishing, 1976), passim.
31. Karl Kaiser, Forschungsinstitut der Deutschen Gesellschaft für Auswärtige Politik (Bonn); Winston Lorn, Council on Foreign Relations (New York); Thierry de Montbriat, Institut Français des Relations Internationales (Paris): David Watt, Royal Institute of International Affairs (London). Published by the Council on Foreign Relations, New York, 1981.
32. Ibid., p. 48.
33. Ibid., p. 40.
34. See also USICA, *Research Memorandum*, January 16, 1981, Tables 5 and 6.
35. Karl W. Deutsch and Richard L. Merritt, "Effects of Events on National and International Images," in *International Behavior*, ed. Herbert C. Kelman (New York: Holt, Rinehart and Winston, 1965), pp. 137-87.
36. James Reston, "The Troubled Alliance," *The Times-Picayune–States-Item* (New Orleans), June 9, 1981, p. 7.
37. Quoted by Reston, "The Troubled Alliance."
38. In this connection, see the comments made by Chancellor Schmidt on this issue insisting again on early negotiations. *Relay from Bonn*, "Chancellor Helmut Schmidt Discusses Security Policy," July 6, 1981.

# APPENDIX A

## TABLE A.1: Certification of Telecasts, Europe and America

| Market Area (billable telecasts) | Station | Network Affiliation | Time of Showing | Date of Showing | Time Class* | Time Value (in $) | TV Homes in Area or CATV Subscribers | Estimated Viewers (numbers and percent) |
|---|---|---|---|---|---|---|---|---|
| Binghamton, N.Y. | WBJA | ABC | 10:30 am | Oct. 5 | C | 142 | 203,300 | 13,800 (7) |
| Dethan, Ala. | WDHN | ABC | 3:30 pm | Oct. 12 | C | 121 | 94,800 | 15,600 (16) |
| Chattanooga, Tenn. | WRIP | Independent | 1:00 pm | Oct. 5 | B | 80 | 375,000 | 43,100 (11) |
| Fort Wayne, Ind. | WFFT | Independent | 7:30 am | Apr. 22 | — | — | 321,900 | 21,900 (7) |
| Grand Rapids-Kalamazoo | WZZM | ABC | 6:30 am | Sep. 7 | C | 832 | 479,500 | 25,900 (5) |
| Casper, Wyo. | KTWO | CBS-NBC-ABC | 11:00 am | Aug. 12 | B | 510 | 75,100 | 20,300 (27) |
| Twin Falls, Id. | KMVT | CBS-NBC-ABC | 11:06 am | Oct. 9 | C | 202 | 39,100 | 10,600 (27) |
| Palm Springs, Calif. | KPLM | ABC | 9:00 am | Sep. 6 | C | 227 | 62,700 | 8,500 (14) |
| Kingsport, Tenn. | CATV | Independent | 8:30 pm | Oct. 5 | — | — | 12,000 | 600 (5) |
| Winston-Salem, N.C. | CATV | Independent | 10:00 am | Oct. 18 | — | — | 18,900 | 6,100 (32) |
| Dillon, Colo. | CATV | Independent | 8:00 am | Sep. 1 | — | — | 5,000 | 1,600 (32) |
| Lafayette, La. | CATV | Independent | 3:00 pm | Oct. 17 | — | — | 5,400 | 600 (11) |
| Ellicott City, Md. | CATV | Independent | 8:00 pm | Aug. 22 | — | — | 1,000 | 100 (10) |

*Time a NATO film was presented. A is prime time; B and C are lower classifications.
Source: North Atlantic Treaty Organization, No. 1557, Cert. No. 31, p. 1, A/E RAL, Oct. 31, 1978.

TABLE A.2: Certification of Telecasts, Europe and America: New Version

| Market Area (billable telecasts) | Station | Network Affiliation | Time of Showing | Date of Showing | Time Class | Time Value (in $) | TV Homes in Area or CATV Subscribers | Estimated Viewers (numbers and percent) |
|---|---|---|---|---|---|---|---|---|
| Columbus, Ohio | WRNS | CBS | 6:30 am | Sep. 25 | C | 700 | 993,100 | 67,500 ( 7) |
| Columbus, Miss. | WCBI | CBS-NBC-ABC | 1:30 pm | Sep. 24 | C | 284 | 177,000 | 90,800 (51) |
| Memphis, Tenn. | WPTY | Independent | 7:00 am | Sep. 16 | — | — | 561,300 | 30,300 ( 3) |
| Baton Rouge, La. | WLPB | Public | 5:00 pm | Sep. 16 | — | — | 80,000 | 2,000 ( 2) |
| Minneapolis, Minn. | WTCN | Independent | 7:30 am | Oct. 9 | D | 600 | 1,062,400 | 57,400 ( 5) |
| Helena, Mont. | DTCM | NBC-ABC | 6:30 pm | Sep. 29 | A | 252 | 13,300 | 2,510 (19) |
| Fairbanks, Alaska | KTVF | CBS | 3:30 pm | Sep. 10 | B | 126 | 17,100 | 2,800 (16) |
| Eureka, Calif. | DVIO | NBC-ABC | 4:30 pm | Oct. 7 | A | 156 | 57,700 | 9,300 (16) |
| Somerset, Kent. | CATV | Independent | 8:30 am | Sep. 12 | — | — | 7,200 | 2,300 (32) |
| Lafayette, La. | CATV | Independent | 1:30 pm | Oct. 9 | — | — | 5,400 | 600 (11) |
| Oakland, Calif. | CATV | Independent | 1:30 pm | Sep. 21 | — | — | 23,200 | 2,700 (12) |
| Knoxville, Tenn. | CATV | Modern CBL | | Oct. 2 | — | — | 6,000 | 800 (13) |
| Westfield, Mass. | CATV | Modern CBL | | Oct. 2 | — | — | 8,000 | 900 (11) |
| Meliourme, Fla. | CATV | Modern CBL | | Oct. 2 | — | — | 23,510 | 2,700 (11) |

| | | | | | |
|---|---|---|---|---|---|
| Peoria, Ill. | CATV | Modern CBL | Oct. 2 | 23,000 | 2,600 (11) |
| Walnut Creek, Calif. | CATV | Modern CBL | Oct. 2 | 16,500 | 1,900 (12) |
| Kansas City, Kans. | CATV | Modern CBL | Oct. 9 | 6,000 | 700 (12) |
| Spencer, Iowa | CATV | Modern CBL | Oct. 9 | 2,300 | 300 (12) |
| Huntington, W.Va. | CATV | Modern CBL | Oct. 9 | 8,000 | 900 (11) |
| Joplin, Mont. | CATV | Modern CBL | Oct. 9 | 4,100 | 500 (12) |
| Plainview, Tex. | CATV | Modern CBL | Oct. 16 | 4,000 | 500 (13) |
| Romeoville, Ill. | CATV | Modern CBL | Oct. 16 | 5,000 | 600 (12) |
| Pt. Pleasant, Wyo. | CATV | Modern CBL | Oct. 16 | 5,000 | 600 (12) |
| Albany, N.Y. | CATV | Modern CBL | Oct. 16 | 25,000 | 2,900 (12) |
| Schenectady, N.Y. | CATV | Modern CBL | Oct. 16 | 16,000 | 1,800 (11) |
| Central Islip, N.Y. | CATV | Modern CBL | Oct. 23 | 65,170 | 7,500 (12) |
| Woodward, Okla. | CATV | Modern CBL | Oct. 23 | 3,600 | 400 (11) |
| Overland Park, Kans. | CATV | Modern CBL | Oct. 23 | 16,400 | 1,900 (12) |
| Kenova, Wyo. | CATV | Modern CBL | Oct. 23 | 5,000 | 600 (12) |
| Meadville, Pa. | CATV | Modern CBL | Oct. 30 | 10,000 | 1,200 (12) |
| Moline, Ill. | CATV | Modern CBL | Oct. 30 | 22,000 | 2,500 (11) |
| Lawrenceburg, Ind. | CATV | Modern CBL | Oct. 30 | 2,300 | 300 (13) |
| Augusta, Me. | CATV | Modern CBL | Oct. 30 | 7,500 | 900 (12) |

Source: North Atlantic Treaty Organization, No. 1557, Cert. No. 9, p. 1, PO2 A/E PAK, Oct. 31, 1978.

## TABLE A.3: Certification of Telecasts: The Great Highway

| Market Area (billable telecasts) | Station | Network Affiliation | Time of Showing | Date of Showing | Time Class | Time Value (in $) | TV Homes in Area or CATV Subscribers | Estimated Viewers (numbers and percent) |
|---|---|---|---|---|---|---|---|---|
| Hickory, N.C. | WHKY | Independent | 4:00 pm | Sep 30 | B | 50 | 62,500 | 32,100 (51) |
| Bowling Green, Ky. | WBKO | ABC | 1:30 pm | Apr 1 | C | 161 | 126,900 | 65,100 (51) |
| Chico-Redding, Calif. | KHSL | CBS | 6:30 pm | Sep 24 | AA | 283 | 167,100 | 85,700 (51) |
| Sacramento, Calif. | KTXL | Independent | 6:00 am | Sep 15 | — | — | 812,600 | 33,300 (4) |
| Sikfston, Mo. | CATV | Independent | 2:00 pm | Sep 20 | — | — | 4,000 | 300 (8) |
| Molino, Ill. | CATV | Independent | 4:00 pm | Oct 12 | — | — | 17,000 | 2,000 (12) |
| Sioux Falls, S.D. | CATV | Independent | 6:30 pm | Oct 11 | — | — | 5,000 | 300 (6) |
| Lafayette, La. | CATV | Independent | 2:30 pm | Sep 25 | — | — | 5,400 | 600 (11) |
| Dillon, Colo. | CATV | Independent | 8:00 am | Jul 31 | — | — | 5,000 | 1,600 (32) |
| Lexington, Va. | CATV | Modern CBL | | Oct 2 | — | — | 2,000 | 200 (10) |
| Rome, Ga. | CATV | Modern CBL | | Oct 2 | — | — | 15,140 | 1,700 (11) |
| Grand Rapids Mich. | CATV | Modern CBL | | Oct 2 | — | — | 20,000 | 2,300 (12) |
| Ephrata, Pa. | CATV | Modern CBL | | Oct 2 | — | — | 6,700 | 800 (12) |
| Danbury, Conn. | CATV | Modern CBL | | Oct 9 | — | — | 13,290 | 1,500 (11) |
| Eatontown, N.J. | CATV | Modern CBL | | Oct 9 | — | — | 3,500 | 400 (11) |

| Market Area (billable telecasts) | Station | Network Affiliation | Time of Showing | Date of Showing | Time Class | Time Value (in $) | TV Homes in Area or CATV Subscribers | Estimated Viewers (numbers and percent) |
|---|---|---|---|---|---|---|---|---|
| Westbrook, Me. | CATV | Modern CBL | | Oct 9 | — | — | 2,000 | 200 (10) |
| Garned, N.C. | CATV | Modern CBL | | Oct 9 | — | — | 8,000 | 900 (11) |
| Hibfing, Minn. | CATV | Modern CBL | | Oct 16 | — | — | 3,670 | 400 (11) |
| Appleton, Wisc. | CATV | Modern CBL | | Oct 16 | — | — | 6,500 | 700 (11) |
| Norman, Okla. | CATV | Modern CBL | | Oct 16 | — | — | 5,000 | 600 (12) |
| Gainseville, Fla. | CATV | Modern CBL | | Oct 16 | — | — | 24,000 | 2,800 (12) |
| St. Albans, Wyo. | CATV | Modern CBL | | Oct 23 | — | — | 5,000 | 600 (12) |
| Plainville, Conn. | CATV | Modern CBL | | Oct 23 | — | — | 12,400 | 1,400 (11) |
| Madisonville, Ky. | CATV | Modern CBL | | Oct 23 | — | — | 9,000 | 1,000 (11) |
| New Bedford, Mass. | CATV | Modern CBL | | Oct 23 | — | — | 5,000 | 600 (12) |
| Reading, Pa. | CATV | Modern CBL | | Oct 30 | — | — | 34,250 | 3,900 (11) |
| Racine, Wisc. | CATV | Modern CBL | | Oct 30 | — | — | 14,100 | 1,600 (11) |
| Springfield, Ill. | CATV | Modern CBL | | Oct 30 | — | — | 22,000 | 2,500 (11) |
| Orlando, Fla. | CATV | Modern CBL | | Oct 30 | — | — | 24,000 | 2,800 (12) |

Source: North Atlantic Treaty Organization, No. 1557, Cert. No. 12, p. 1, R/E RAK, Oct. 31, 1978.

# APPENDIX B

## QUESTIONNAIRE

The following set of questions ranges over a wide area of concerns dealing with domestic and foreign policy issues. You will probably find some items more interesting than others. On some questions, you may have no opinion at all. If so, just go on to the next item. Note that there are no questions of a personal nature about your background and your responses are strictly confidential. They will be used only in statistical summaries.

First of all, we are going to list some things people tell us when we talk with them. Read the following statements and tell us whether you agree or disagree.

1. "People like me don't have any say about what government does."

    Agree          Disagree

2. "Voting is the only way that people like me can have any say about how the government runs things."

    Agree          Disagree

3. "Sometimes politics and government seem so complicated that a person like me can't really understand what's going on."

    Agree          Disagree

4. "I don't think public officials care much what people like me think."

    Agree          Disagree

5. "Generally speaking, those we elect to Congress lose touch with the people pretty quickly."

    Agree          Disagree

6. "Political parties are only interested in people's votes but not in their opinions."

    Agree          Disagree

We are faced with many problems in this country, none of which can be solved easily or inexpensively. I'm going to name some of these problems, and for each one I'd like you to tell me whether you think we're spending too much money on it, too little money, or about the right amount. First (READ ITEM 7) . . . are we spending too much, too little, or about the right amount on (ITEM)?

7. Research and science

    RESPONSE

    Too little                          _____
    About right                         _____
    Too much                            _____
    Don't know                          _____
    No answer                           _____

8. Improving and protecting the environment

    RESPONSE

    Too little                          _____
    About right                         _____
    Too much                            _____
    Don't know                          _____
    No answer                           _____

9. Improving and protecting the nation's health

    RESPONSE

    Too little                          _____
    About right                         _____
    Too much                            _____
    Don't know                          _____
    No answer                           _____

10. Solving the problems of the big cities

    RESPONSE

    Too little                          _____
    About right                         _____
    Too much                            _____
    Don't know                          _____
    No answer                           _____

11. Halting the rising crime rate

    RESPONSE

    Too little   _____
    About right  _____
    Too much     _____
    Don't know   _____
    No answer    _____

12. Dealing with drug addiction

    RESPONSE

    Too little   _____
    About right  _____
    Too much     _____
    Don't know   _____
    No answer    _____

13. Improving the nation's educational system

    RESPONSE

    Too little   _____
    About right  _____
    Too much     _____
    Don't know   _____
    No answer    _____

14. (Question deleted)

15. The military, armaments, and defense

    RESPONSE

    Too little   _____
    About right  _____
    Too much     _____
    Don't know   _____
    No answer    _____

16. Foreign aid

    RESPONSE

    Too little   _____
    About right  _____
    Too much     _____
    Don't know   _____
    No answer    _____

17. Social costs

    RESPONSE

    Too little             _____
    About right            _____
    Too much               _____
    Don't know             _____
    No answer              _____

At this point, we would like to ask you some questions about America's standing in the world and get some of your ideas about international relations.

18. How about the chances of our country getting into war? Would you say that at the present time you are:

    a. Pretty worried about the possibility of our getting into another war.

    b. Somewhat worried about the possibility of our getting into another war.

    c. Not worried at all about the possibility of our getting into another war.

19. Since the end of World War II, the U.S. has kept an army in Europe to help defend our NATO allies. In order to further the interest of peace should we:

    a. Return American troops to the U.S.

    b. Keep about the same number over there as now.

    c. Send over more troops than at present.

20. The Senate is currently debating ratification of the Strategic Arms Limitation Treaty (SALT II) which President Carter and Soviet President Brezhnev signed in Vienna some months ago. What do you think the wisest thing the Senate could do to aid the cause of peace?

    a. Okay the treaty as it is.

    b. Okay the treaty with some reservations and amendments.

    c. Reject the treaty entirely.

Here are some more statements we hear from various people we talk to. Indicate to what extent you agree or disagree with these statements.

21. The United States must be willing to run any risk of war which may be necessary to prevent the spread of communism.

    Agree Strongly    Agree Somewhat    Disagree Somewhat    Disagree Strongly    Not sure

22. If disarmament negotiations are not successful, the United States should begin a gradual program of unilateral disarmament—i.e., disarm whether other countries do or not.

    Agree Strongly    Agree Somewhat    Disagree Somewhat    Disagree Strongly    Not sure

23. Pacifist demonstrations—picketing missile bases, peace walks, etc.—are harmful to the best interest of the American people.

    Agree Strongly    Agree Somewhat    Disagree Somewhat    Disagree Strongly    Not sure

24. The United States has no moral principles to carry its struggle against communism to the point of risking the destruction of the human race.

    Agree Strongly    Agree Somewhat    Disagree Somewhat    Disagree Strongly    Not sure

25. It is contrary to my moral principles to participate in war and the killing of other people.

    Agree Strongly    Agree Somewhat    Disagree Somewhat    Disagree Strongly    Not sure

26. The real enemy today is no longer communism but rather war itself.

    Agree Strongly    Agree Somewhat    Disagree Somewhat    Disagree Strongly    Not sure

27. Pacifism is simply not a practical philosophy in the world today.

    Agree Strongly    Agree Somewhat    Disagree Somewhat    Disagree Strongly    Not sure

28. There has been a lot of discussion in the news lately about defense in the United States. Some people say that without an alliance like NATO the defense of the U.S. would be greatly weakened. Others argue, however, that military blocs like NATO hurt the cause of peace. How do you view this problem?

   a. The United States would be weaker without NATO.

   b. Blocs like NATO threaten peace.

29. To take the argument further some people say that the Europeans should defend themselves without U.S. help, while others say that NATO, our alliance with them, helps defend our way of life. How do you view this?

   a. The Europeans should fend for themselves.

   b. NATO helps protect our way of life.

30. It is often said that freedom is the most precious item in our society. However, others contend that freedom should give way to the assurance of social justice and full equality. Which of the following statements comes closest to your view?

   a. Freedom must always have the highest priority.

   b. The assurance of social justice and equality must always have the highest priority.

   c. Without the assurance of freedom, social justice and equality may not be very meaningful.

Below is a list of countries with which the United States has to deal in today's world. Opposite each country is a scale from the highest position of +5 for a country which you like very much, to the lowest position of −5 for a country you dislike very much. How far up the scale or how far down the scale would you rate the following countries:   (Like) +5 +4 +3 +2 +1 −1 −2 −3 −4 −5 (Dislike)

|  | | |
|---|---|---|
| Russia | −5 −4 −3 −2 −1 | +1 +2 +3 +4 +5 |
| Japan | −5 −4 −3 −2 −1 | +1 +2 +3 +4 +5 |
| England | −5 −4 −3 −2 −1 | +1 +2 +3 +4 +5 |
| Canada | −5 −4 −3 −2 −1 | +1 +2 +3 +4 +5 |
| Brazil | −5 −4 −3 −2 −1 | +1 +2 +3 +4 +5 |
| China (Peking) | −5 −4 −3 −2 −1 | +1 +2 +3 +4 +5 |
| Israel | −5 −4 −3 −2 −1 | +1 +2 +3 +4 +5 |
| Egypt | −5 −4 −3 −2 −1 | +1 +2 +3 +4 +5 |
| France | −5 −4 −3 −2 −1 | +1 +2 +3 +4 +5 |

| | | |
|---|---|---|
| Italy | −5 −4 −3 −2 −1 | +1 +2 +3 +4 +5 |
| Poland | −5 −4 −3 −2 −1 | +1 +2 +3 +4 +5 |
| West Germany | −5 −4 −3 −2 −1 | +1 +2 +3 +4 +5 |
| Holland | −5 −4 −3 −2 −1 | +1 +2 +3 +4 +5 |
| East Germany | −5 −4 −3 −2 −1 | +1 +2 +3 +4 +5 |
| Mexico | −5 −4 −3 −2 −1 | +1 +2 +3 +4 +5 |
| Saudi Arabia | −5 −4 −3 −2 −1 | +1 +2 +3 +4 +5 |
| Belgium | −5 −4 −3 −2 −1 | +1 +2 +3 +4 +5 |
| Iran | −5 −4 −3 −2 −1 | +1 +2 +3 +4 +5 |
| Sweden | −5 −4 −3 −2 −1 | +1 +2 +3 +4 +5 |
| Spain | −5 −4 −3 −2 −1 | +1 +2 +3 +4 +5 |
| Portugal | −5 −4 −3 −2 −1 | +1 +2 +3 +4 +5 |
| Norway | −5 −4 −3 −2 −1 | +1 +2 +3 +4 +5 |
| Switzerland | −5 −4 −3 −2 −1 | +1 +2 +3 +4 +5 |
| Denmark | −5 −4 −3 −2 −1 | +1 +2 +3 +4 +5 |

Now we have a question about something you may or may not have heard about. Which of the following countries are members of NATO and, thus, allies of the United States?

| | | |
|---|---|---|
| Canada | Ally | Not an Ally |
| Mexico | Ally | Not an Ally |
| Luxembourg | Ally | Not an Ally |
| Iceland | Ally | Not an Ally |
| Switzerland | Ally | Not an Ally |
| Portugal | Ally | Not an Ally |
| Turkey | Ally | Not an Ally |
| Greece | Ally | Not an Ally |
| Sweden | Ally | Not an Ally |
| Denmark | Ally | Not an Ally |
| England | Ally | Not an Ally |
| Italy | Ally | Not an Ally |
| Spain | Ally | Not an Ally |
| West Germany | Ally | Not an Ally |

# APPENDIX C

## SHOULD THE U.S SUPPLY MILITARY FORCE IF THE SOVIET UNION ATTACKED . . .

| | Weighted Base- Total Sample | Age | | | | Education | | | Region | | | |
|---|---|---|---|---|---|---|---|---|---|---|---|---|
| | | 18-29 | 30-49 | 50-64 | 65 & older | Col- lege | High School | Grade School | East | Mid- west | South | West |
| **Weighted Base- Total Sample** | | | | | | | | | | | | |
| Number | 1,525 | 412 | 556 | 316 | 205 | 542 | 687 | 288 | 413 | 444 | 413 | 255 |
| Percent | 100 | 100 | 100 | 100 | 100 | 100 | 100 | 100 | 100 | 100 | 100 | 100 |
| **Canada** | | | | | | | | | | | | |
| Should | | | | | | | | | | | | |
| Number | 1,323 | 355 | 509 | 270 | 160 | 508 | 586 | 221 | 356 | 393 | 344 | 230 |
| Percent | 86.8 | 86.2 | 91.5 | 85.4 | 78.0 | 93.7 | 85.3 | 76.7 | 86.2 | 88.5 | 83.3 | 90.2 |
| Should not | | | | | | | | | | | | |
| Number | 80 | 26 | 20 | 18 | 14 | 14 | 37 | 29 | 24 | 25 | 23 | 8 |
| Percent | 5.2 | 6.3 | 3.6 | 5.7 | 6.4 | 2.6 | 5.4 | 10.1 | 5.8 | 5.6 | 5.6 | 3.1 |
| Don't know | | | | | | | | | | | | |
| Number | 122 | 31 | 27 | 28 | 31 | 20 | 64 | 38 | 33 | 26 | 46 | 17 |
| Percent | 8.0 | 7.5 | 4.9 | 8.9 | 15.1 | 3.7 | 9.3 | 13.2 | 8.0 | 5.9 | 11.1 | 6.7 |

|  | | | | | | | | | | | | |
|---|---|---|---|---|---|---|---|---|---|---|---|---|
| **France** | | | | | | | | | | | | |
| Should | | | | | | | | | | | | |
| Number | 913 | 267 | 369 | 165 | 94 | 372 | 398 | 137 | 241 | 260 | 252 | 160 |
| Percent | 59.9 | 64.8 | 66.4 | 52.2 | 45.9 | 68.6 | 57.9 | 47.6 | 58.4 | 58.6 | 61.0 | 62.7 |
| Should not | | | | | | | | | | | | |
| Number | 327 | 93 | 102 | 87 | 38 | 115 | 145 | 67 | 91 | 113 | 69 | 54 |
| Percent | 21.4 | 22.6 | 18.3 | 27.5 | 18.5 | 21.2 | 21.1 | 23.3 | 22.0 | 25.5 | 16.7 | 21.2 |
| Don't know | | | | | | | | | | | | |
| Number | 285 | 52 | 85 | 64 | 73 | 55 | 144 | 84 | 81 | 71 | 92 | 41 |
| Percent | 18.7 | 12.6 | 15.3 | 20.3 | 35.6 | 10.1 | 21.0 | 29.2 | 19.6 | 16.0 | 22.3 | 16.1 |
| **England** | | | | | | | | | | | | |
| Should | | | | | | | | | | | | |
| Number | 1,157 | 313 | 462 | 222 | 135 | 452 | 517 | 180 | 306 | 330 | 315 | 206 |
| Percent | 75.9 | 76.0 | 83.1 | 70.3 | 65.9 | 83.4 | 75.3 | 62.5 | 74.1 | 74.3 | 76.3 | 80.8 |
| Should not | | | | | | | | | | | | |
| Number | 176 | 61 | 47 | 46 | 18 | 54 | 82 | 40 | 52 | 63 | 34 | 27 |
| Percent | 11.5 | 14.8 | 8.5 | 14.6 | 8.8 | 10.0 | 11.9 | 13.9 | 12.6 | 14.2 | 8.2 | 10.6 |
| Don't know | | | | | | | | | | | | |
| Number | 192 | 38 | 47 | 48 | 52 | 36 | 88 | 68 | 55 | 51 | 64 | 22 |
| Percent | 12.6 | 9.2 | 8.5 | 15.2 | 25.4 | 6.6 | 12.8 | 23.6 | 13.3 | 11.5 | 15.5 | 8.6 |

| | | | | | | | | | | | | |
|---|---|---|---|---|---|---|---|---|---|---|---|---|
| **Japan** | | | | | | | | | | | | |
| *Should* | | | | | | | | | | | | |
| Number | 871 | 249 | 368 | 160 | 78 | 375 | 387 | 107 | 244 | 238 | 234 | 155 |
| Percent | 57.1 | 60.4 | 66.2 | 50.6 | 38.0 | 69.2 | 56.2 | 36.8 | 59.1 | 53.6 | 56.7 | 60.8 |
| *Should not* | | | | | | | | | | | | |
| Number | 394 | 122 | 108 | 96 | 57 | 113 | 181 | 96 | 100 | 136 | 91 | 67 |
| Percent | 25.8 | 29.6 | 19.4 | 30.4 | 27.8 | 20.8 | 26.3 | 33.3 | 24.2 | 30.6 | 22.0 | 26.3 |
| *Don't know* | | | | | | | | | | | | |
| Number | 260 | 41 | 80 | 60 | 70 | 54 | 120 | 86 | 69 | 70 | 88 | 33 |
| Percent | 17.0 | 10.0 | 14.4 | 19.0 | 34.1 | 10.0 | 17.5 | 29.9 | 16.7 | 15.8 | 21.3 | 12.9 |
| **Saudia Arabia** | | | | | | | | | | | | |
| *Should* | | | | | | | | | | | | |
| Number | 686 | 195 | 274 | 133 | 72 | 322 | 274 | 86 | 199 | 177 | 186 | 124 |
| Percent | 45.0 | 47.3 | 49.3 | 42.1 | 35.1 | 59.4 | 39.9 | 29.9 | 48.2 | 39.9 | 45.0 | 48.6 |
| *Should not* | | | | | | | | | | | | |
| Number | 558 | 168 | 184 | 128 | 66 | 160 | 269 | 126 | 148 | 195 | 133 | 82 |
| Percent | 36.6 | 40.8 | 33.1 | 50.5 | 32.2 | 29.5 | 39.2 | 43.8 | 35.8 | 43.9 | 32.2 | 32.2 |
| *Don't know* | | | | | | | | | | | | |
| Number | 281 | 49 | 98 | 55 | 67 | 60 | 144 | 76 | 66 | 72 | 84 | 49 |
| Percent | 18.4 | 11.9 | 17.6 | 17.4 | 32.7 | 11.1 | 21.0 | 26.4 | 16.0 | 16.2 | 22.8 | 19.2 |

| | | | | | | | | | | | | |
|---|---|---|---|---|---|---|---|---|---|---|---|---|
| Israel | | | | | | | | | | | | |
| Should | | | | | | | | | | | | |
| Number | 842 | 236 | 338 | 153 | 98 | 343 | 357 | 139 | 228 | 220 | 259 | 135 |
| Percent | 55.2 | 57.3 | 60.8 | 48.4 | 47.8 | 63.3 | 52.0 | 48.3 | 55.2 | 49.5 | 62.7 | 52.9 |
| Should not | | | | | | | | | | | | |
| Number | 457 | 140 | 140 | 112 | 53 | 147 | 215 | 90 | 134 | 153 | 89 | 81 |
| Percent | 30.0 | 34.0 | 25.2 | 35.4 | 25.9 | 27.1 | 31.3 | 31.3 | 32.4 | 34.5 | 21.5 | 31.8 |
| Don't know | | | | | | | | | | | | |
| Number | 226 | 36 | 78 | 51 | 54 | 52 | 115 | 49 | 51 | 71 | 65 | 39 |
| Percent | 14.8 | 8.7 | 14.0 | 16.1 | 26.3 | 9.6 | 16.7 | 20.5 | 12.3 | 16.0 | 15.7 | 15.3 |
| Turkey | | | | | | | | | | | | |
| Should | | | | | | | | | | | | |
| Number | 551 | 162 | 232 | 103 | 47 | 231 | 244 | 74 | 153 | 152 | 154 | 92 |
| Percent | 36.1 | 39.3 | 41.7 | 32.6 | 22.9 | 42.6 | 35.5 | 25.7 | 37.0 | 34.2 | 37.3 | 36.1 |
| Should not | | | | | | | | | | | | |
| Number | 619 | 191 | 197 | 139 | 75 | 225 | 282 | 107 | 176 | 199 | 135 | 109 |
| Percent | 40.6 | 46.4 | 35.4 | 44.0 | 36.6 | 41.5 | 41.0 | 37.2 | 42.6 | 44.8 | 32.7 | 42.7 |
| Don't know | | | | | | | | | | | | |
| Number | 355 | 59 | 127 | 74 | 83 | 86 | 161 | 107 | 84 | 93 | 124 | 54 |
| Percent | 23.3 | 14.3 | 22.8 | 23.4 | 40.5 | 15.9 | 23.4 | 37.2 | 20.3 | 20.9 | 30.0 | 21.2 |

*Note:* Percentages are rounded.
*Source:* Gallup Organization, Inc., Questions 3-5 on 824/825P October 1980.

# INDEX

Aaron, Raymond, 107
Adler, Kenneth P., and Wertman, Douglas A., 123
Allen, Richard, 88
Allison, Graham, 127
Angola, 138
Atlantic Council of the United States, 65, 79
Atlantic defense relationship, 2
Atlantic Institute for International Affairs, 14

Backfire bomber, 129
Basic Law of the Federal Republic of Germany, 136
Belgium: 10, 13, 137; missile approval, 129; party affiliation, 117, 120; U.S. public opinion toward, 59, 88, 104
Brandt, Willi, 67-68, 136
Brazil, 72, 74
Britain: 10, 19; defense spending, 102-4, 127; education, 113; neutralism, 104, 114, 120-21; occupation, 112-14; party affiliation, 111, 114, 121-22, 129-30, 139; U.S. public opinion toward, 90, 92, 100, 102, 104-5, 108; viewed from EC, 97, 99; viewed from U.S., 72, 82-83
Bulgaria, 16
Bundy, McGeorge, 130

Canada: 2, 72, 82-83, 131; U.S. public opinion toward, 59
Cable Television (CATV), 46
Carter, Jimmy, 14, 26-27, 33, 35, 68, 77, 83, 143
Caterpillar firm, 138
Ceauscescu, Nicolae, 30

Cheysson, Claude, 104, 112
Chicago Council on Foreign Relations (CCFR), 65-66, 75, 87
China, Peoples Republic of: relations with U.S., 16; relations with USSR, 16; viewed from EC, 90-91; viewed from U.S., 59, 72-73
Chrysler, 27
Clausewitz, Carl von, 75, 110
Conference on Security and Cooperation in Europe (CSCE), 135, 140
Corterier, Peter, 14-15
Cramer's V, 71, 111, 113-14
Cuba, 68, 75
Czechoslovakia: 126, 135; dissidence in, 16

de Gaulle, Charles, 5, 10-11, 13, 15
Denmark, 13
Detente, 2, 12, 15, 112, 134
Deutch, Karl, 142
Dragon weapons system, 7
Dulles, John Foster, 4, 18

East Germany: 27, 68, 136; U.S. public opinion toward, 59
Egypt, viewed from U.S., 72, 74
Eisenhower, Dwight, 4, 18
El Salvador, 14
Ethiopia, 138
European Community (EC), 90, 91, 138, 140
Euro-American alliance, 99, 111
Eurobarometer, 91
Eurohawks-Eurodoves, 106, 108-9, 111, 113, 116, 123, 133
European Defense Community, 8
European Political Cooperation (EPC), 140
Eurostrategic weapons, 13-14

Final Act, 135, 140
Finlandization, 3-4, 102-3, 106, 108
Ford, Gerald, 2, 135
Foreign Policy Association, (FPA), 65-66
François-Poncet, Jean, 15
France: 15, 19, 82-83; defense spendings, 102-3, 127; Gaullism, 99, 107, 116, 132; interventionism, 107; isolationism, 99; neutralism, 120-21; nuclear weapons, 8, 10; party affiliation, 116; relations with West Germany, 10; U.S. public opinion toward, 92, 100, 102, 104-5, 108-9, 120; viewed from EC, 97-99
free world, 66, 73

Gallup polls, 65-66, 75, 79-80, 132
Genscher, Hans Dietrich, 129
German Allensbach Institute, 121-22
German Social Democratic Party, 14
Gouré, Leon, 7
Greece, 2, 27, 30, 33-35, 44, 82
ground-launched cruise missile (GLCM), 6-7, 112

Haig, Alexander, 24
Harmel Report, 134
Helsinki Accords, 16
HOT (Haute subsonic Optiquement téléguidé tiré d'un Tube) weapons system, 7

ICBMs, 6-7, 10, 14
Interuniversity Consortium for Political and Social Research (ICPSR), 91
Iran, 16, 71, 75, 105
Israel: 75, 140; viewed from U.S., 72, 74, 82-83

Italy: 10; and LRTNF, 129; party affiliation, 111, 117; U.S. public opinion toward, 59, 90, 104

Japan: 16; U.S. public opinion toward, 59; viewed from EC, 97; viewed from U.S., 72, 74, 82-83
Jervis, Robert, 19

Kennedy, John F., 4
Kincade, William H., 8
Kissinger, Henry, 18, 135
Korean War, 97
Kyd, David, 23

Lance missiles, 7
Lenin, Vladimir, warning of capitalist encirclement, 16
Lewis, Kevin N., 6
Lomé Convention, 138
long-range theater nuclear forces (LRTNF), 106, 121, 123, 129, 134, 136, 143
Luttwak, Edward, 6, 8, 110
Luxembourg, 128

Mansfield, Mike, 131
Marshall Plan, 1
Merritt, Richard, 142
Mexico, 60
Middleton, Drew, 24
MILAN (Missile d'Infanterie Leger Antichar), weapons system, 7
Mitterrand, François, 104, 116, 143
mutual and balanced force reductions (MBFR), 135
mutually assured destruction (MAD), 4, 8

National Archives, 91
National Congress of Evangelical Churches, 126
National Opinion Research Center (NORC): 53, 65; General Social Survey, 65-66, 68
NATO: 1, 3; comparative military strength, 11; Council Report on the Future Tasks of the Alliance, 134; Information Service, 22, 32, 45; news coverage of, 24-25, 32; Nuclear Planning Group, 139; Press Service, 24; publications of, 24; thirty-year anniversary of, 30-31
Netherlands: 4, 13, 35, 137; missile approval, 129; party affiliation, 120, 139; U.S. public opinion toward, 88, 104
New International Economic Order, 139
Nixon, Richard, 18, 46, 135
North-South relations, 68-70, 79, 138
Norway, 13

*Ostpolitik*, 15, 136
Ottawa Summit, 137, 139, 143

Pakistan, 16
Panama Canal, 75
Pershing II missile, 6-7, 13, 87, 129
Persian Gulf, 17, 83, 105, 142
piggybacking, 91
Poland: 68, 122, 138; labor strife in, 16-17; viewed from U.S., 59
Presidential Directive 59, 8
Public Broadcasting System (PBS), 46

Rathjens, George, 4

Reagan administration, 68, 77, 88, 110, 135, 137, 140, 142-44
Reston, James, 143
Rhodesia, 75
Romania: 30; independence of, 16
Roosevelt, Franklin, 18
Roosevelt, Theodore, 57
Ruina, Jack, 4

SALT talks, 11-14, 143
Saudi Arabia: U.S. public opinion toward, 59; viewed from U.S., 82-83
Schlesinger, James, 5
Schmidt, Helmut, 3, 13-14, 34, 129-30
Shaw, George Bernard, 113
South Yemen, 139
Soviet hawk-dove hypothesis, 13
Soviet relations with: Bulgaria, 16; China, 16; Czechoslovakia, 16; Islam, 16-17; Poland, 16; Romania, 16; Satellites, 137
Soviet Union: 2-4; defense spending, 102-3; expansionism-hegemony, 16, 138; GNP, 17; Islamic minority in, 16; Russophobia, 61
Spain, relations with NATO, 30
SS-20 Missiles, 6-7
standard metropolitan statistical area (SMSA), 45
Sweden, 60
Switzerland: 121; viewed from the EC, 91

theatre nuclear forces (TNF), 13-14; demonstrations against, 126
third world, 73, 79, 138, 140, 142, 144
Thyness, Paul, 11
TOW (Tube-launched Optically-tracked Wire-guided anti-tank missile), 7
Turkey, 1, 16, 27, 30, 34-35, 44, 82-83

United Nations General Assembly, 139, 144
United States: adventurism, 10, 13, 15; arms monopoly, 5; Bureau of Census, 45; crime, 77, 79; defense spending, 102-3; elite opinions, 33, 72; grain embargo, 68, 110; hegemony, 35, 87; indecision, 14; isolationism, 15, 67; media, 23, 25; militarism, 45; nationalism, 14; opinion of communism, 66, 68-70, 79; public opinion, 108-9; regionalism, 82, 90; Republicans vs. Democrats, 111; trade policy, 2
U.S. International Communications Agency (USICA), 91, 107
U.S. relations with: Brazil, 72, 74; Britain, 72, 74, 82-83, 89; Canada, 89; China, 73; EC, 90-91; Egypt, 72, 74; Israel, 72, 74; Japan, 72, 74, 82-83; third world, 79

Vance, Cyrus, 35
Vietnam: generation, 77, 83; war, 18, 71, 86-87

Warsaw Pact, 7, 11-12, 16, 30, 33, 97, 99, 127, 129, 136
Weinberger, Casper, 88
West Berlin, 136
West Germany: 4, 9-10, 19, 35, 43; defense spending, 102-3, 127; party affiliation, 117, 139; relations with Eastern bloc, 14, 27, 105, 136; revanchism, 13; U.S. public opinion toward, 59, 91-92, 100, 102, 104-5, 108-9; viewed from EC, 97
Wittkopf, Eugene, 67

Yugoslavia, 10, 75

# ABOUT THE AUTHORS

WERNER J. FELD is a professor of Political Science at the University of New Orleans. He is the author of numerous publications, including *Transnational Business Collaboration Among Common Market Countries* (1970), *Nongovernmental Forces and World Politics* (1972), *The European Community in World Affairs* (1976), *Domestic Political Realities and European Unification* (with John K. Wildgen) (1976), *International Relations: A Transnational Approach* (with Gavin Boyd) (1979), *Comparative Regional Systems* (1980), and *Western Germany and the European Community* (1981). In addition, Dr. Feld is the author of more than 60 articles in various journals. He received a law degree (Referendar) after attending the University of Berlin and a Ph.D. in Political Science from Tulane University.

This is JOHN K. WILDGEN's second book with Werner Feld on Europe. Five years ago they collaborated on *Domestic Political Realities and European Unification*. Professor Wildgen has had a career-long interest in quantification in comparative politics which, he maintains, is not to be confused with foreign area studies. As a consequence his writings appear not only in journals such as *International Organization, Orbis*, and *Comparative Political Studies*, but also in the *Journal of Politics* and *Legislative Studies Quarterly*. He is currently collaborating with several other political scientists on a study of public opinion in the American South. He is a professor of Political Science at the University of New Orleans, Louisiana. His Ph.D. was earned at Duke University.